CONTENTS

The Parables of the Tail with No Teeth, Part I

The Old Teeth and Tail Switch

Once upon a time, a castle stood in the midst of fertile fields in the Land of Red Tape. It was a mighty castle, perched high upon a wild hill and virtually surrounded by a fruitful river forming a natural moat. Access to this castle was difficult but worthwhile.

The castle had not always been a castle. Once it had been only a stable, but operated by some very young and very smart people. In fact many of them were geniuses—eccentric, but very good at what they did. What they did was very specialized and complicated. A keen intelligence, rigorous training and lots of experience were necessary to do the jobs well. The people that did these jobs were called "Tekees."

Everyone worked hard in the stable producing animals for the kingdom and manure for the neighboring farmers. Business was good and the demand rose for more animals and more manure, so more people had to be hired to become Tekees.

The new Tekees did not share the common background

and experience of the original Tekees. They had to be trained and retrained to do things in the time-honored ways of the stable, since the old Tekees could imagine no other way to produce manure. And so it became clear that running the stable could not just continue to happen in a purely democratic fashion. They needed a hierarchy.

The man who founded the stable, Arthur of Arthritis upon Knee, got himself declared king by his close comrades. The newly minted king appointed all his friends to lead the new hierarchy. Arthur made his son, Arthur the Lesser, Prince of the Piles, with everyday oversight of the stable. The king then knighted every one of his boon buddies and named them Lord Knights of the Conference Table. The rest of the old Tekees were dubbed vassals and made Stewards of the Stalls, middle management. The new Tekees remained peasants doing all the dirty work.

Nearly all of the old Tekees, now lords, were possessed of a fatal flaw. They were at their best when dealing with the animals. They simply loved working with the animals. Unfortunately, they were at their worst when dealing with people. Working with animals was not the same as working with people, or worse, being lords over people. Dealing with people as equals made them very uncomfortable. It was easier just to lord it over them. Furthermore, there was no one to teach the old technicians how to be lords. They were in the same boat and they thought the stable full of sharks.

The lords preferred being around people who liked and

worked well with animals. Therefore, they surrounded themselves with people just like themselves. They promoted people just like themselves and replaced themselves with people just like themselves. They enjoyed this "work" and applied themselves with gusto to building their "empires."

Soon the stable became too crowded because of all the new minions, so the lords asked the king to build a castle. They needed a castle to house all the scribes and scribe supplies now necessary because they had a hierarchy and the many hierarchs in it. The lords also needed a castle to impress the increasing number of visiting officials and farmers who were their customers. Ultimately, the lords needed a castle because they did not want to work in stables, or very near them for that matter, and preferably upwind at that.

After the castle was built and the lords moved in, some of them realized that they were not comfortable there. These lords continued to spend much of their time in the stable working on the animals with the vassals. They didn't teach the vassals now responsible for taking care of the animals, but simply joined into the process themselves. They led by example and monitored progress through constant participation. Of course, the vassals had to perform the tasks the same way the lords had always done, or they were not promoted.

The lords continued to show the talents that made them such great technicians. They invented new styles of horseshoes to be used according to the terrain upon which the cavalry expected to fight. They bred animals according to the attributes necessary to the intended function of them. They even discovered that they could vary the qualities of the manure according to the fodder used. The stable grew in this way and prospered, but mostly it grew. Moreover, as it grew, it became harder and harder for the lords to continue in a participatory mode. Increasingly, they had to rely on others and trust others to do the work. The people who reported to them soon had people reporting to them in turn and then those people had people reporting to them.

Borrowing jargon from the kingdom's cavalry, the vassals who worked in the stable referred to themselves as the *teeth* of the stable, because they were the business end of the endeavor. Those who worked in the castle became known as the *tail*, because they were as far away from the business end as they could get.

The lords then had to change their ways slightly. They did so by creating, and participating in, study groups and task forces that worked on specific animals; those that the lords understood and loved and found aromatically compelling. All other tasks required operating the stable—many of which were necessitated by improvements in the art of warfare as well as a revolution in agronomy—were left to subordinates to accomplish on their own, with little or no support from the lords.

Since the stable was still relatively small, the lords were able to manage effectively in this way, so the supply of animals and manure continued to burgeon. The stable became very popular because of both the quantity and the quality of its products. It cornered the market for the entire kingdom. When customers came to the stable to ask for product improvements or even something entirely new, they were told that the stable was already producing the best and the lords knew best what was good for the customer. And that's what the customer got, nothing more nothing less, no matter what he said or did.

In the good old days the lords had worked closely with their vassals and learned through daily contact who was better than whom. That was not possible anymore. They also had to pay more money to the vassals who possessed the unique skills needed to raise animals and meet the ever-increasing demand for manure. Solutions had to be found for the problems arising from these and other factors and the king had to buy the services of two wise men, named Smoke and Mirrors, from a neighboring kingdom to help him do so.

The Wise Men developed a concept called Transubstantiation, for which a program was instituted to identify the best among the vassals for promotion and possible ennobling as lords. They also created a new hierarchy to administer the program so that the lords would not have to waste time getting involved in the process.

Smoke and Mirrors then invented an arrangement, called the Indenture Program, and designed to ensure the training of vassals chosen for Transubstantiation. Naturally, after a while the indenture program settled into a normal bureaucratic expediency. Lack of attention from the castle eventually resulted in a certain diffidence on the part of the administrators of the program-- not to mention disillusionment among the indentured. Decreasingly less oversight was given and the program lost its luster.

Transubstantiation became a matter of passing a written examination with no personal evaluation by the lords. More and more vassals became Transubstantiated and soon one certificate wasn't enough anymore. A new automatic way of discriminating between vassals was necessary, so the need to diversify was invented. Vassals with two certificates became more sought after than vassals with only one.

Many vassals became professional students and spent more time in the pursuit of certificates than in actually doing any real work. The lords were finally forced to decree that it did not matter what or how many certificates a vassal earned, one was enough. Possessing a certificate was no longer a matter of benefit so much as it was a detriment if one did not have one. The king had to order more trees cut so that the Lord of the Flush could make more paper.

The Wise Men continued to think of new programs and functions. Neither had anything to do with raising animals or distributing manure, but they sounded good to the lords because they justified more people, which in turn justified more towers for the castle.

The old stable had to be expanded and new stables built. Each new stable also meant another new tower for the castle. The towers were built higher and farther away from the stables, as the tail of the stable grew longer. As the lords got used to the castle, they lost their taste (and smell) for the stables. They no longer had anything in common with the vassals, and it was hard to make the trip down to the stables now that they were physically and psychologically so far away.

So many animals had been obtained that it became difficult to dispense the resultant manure. The Wise Men again came to the rescue. Realizing that the problem could be solved by better handling and packaging methods, they called for the automation of the stables. The Wise Men convinced the lords that they needed machines to do the simplest tasks and the preliminary operations in the process. They predicted that not only would the product improve, but that it would do so with no increase in the numbers of vassals.

Therefore, the lords bought machines and built another new wing on the castle to house the hierarchy created by automation. Then the realization dawned, slowly but inexorably, in the stable and in the castle, that the Wise Men had been wrong. Automation did not hold down the number of vassals. Instead, it actually greatly expanded the number of jobs needed to support the machines. In the stables the only people available were vassals, so vassals were encouraged to work with the machines and not with the manure. Eventually the average stable, which once had had ten vassals caring for the animals and processing the manure, now had only five doing those jobs and ten more vassals caring for the machines. The people caring for the machines were given more gold then those caring for the animals which, of course, didn't make it any easier to obtain and retain vassals to care for animals.

The tail became bigger than the teeth. The lords hired as many people as the king would allow, but now they had to settle for vassals from surrounding kingdoms. These vassals were not familiar with the different ways of the kingdom and did not always fit in very well.

Simultaneously, farmers cried that they not only needed more manure, but that they needed it much faster. There weren't enough vassals to process so much manure so fast, and there was no way to acquire more since the king, in disgust, had refused to give the Prince of the Piles any more gold for people. The Wise Men responded to the crisis by devising a system of pipes that transmitted the manure directly from the animal to the farmer's fields. Now the stable was unable to do any preprocessing of the manure so it fell to the farmer to do so.

The universally accepted answer to the growing lack of sufficient manpower was to acquire more machines. So, many more were bought. Soon the castle was filled to capacity with machines and all the new ones had to fit into the stable areas. The only spaces available were those that the vassals occupied so they had to be moved into smaller and smaller cubicles.

More and more money was spent on machines and less and less was available to pay the vassals. Vast staffs had grown up to help the lords try to solve the ever-increasing problems. Large numbers of specialized vassals, called artisans, had to be hired to run the newer machines, and an almost equal number hired just to do the hiring and the buying. Less and less attention was paid to the stable vassals, the best of whom began to desert the stables in alarming numbers and joined those already in the castles.

The Wise Men, ever anxious to justify more of the large amounts of gold they received, devised a new scheme under which the lords were rotated among the castles regularly and often. They never stayed long enough to be identified with a particular stable and left before the consequences of their decisions became obvious. The lords generally coped with this system by either avoiding decisions altogether or making decisions that promised short-term gains. They wished to avoid actions that, no matter how they promised long-term gain, possessed the potential for short-term loss.

The king could not admit he had mistakenly raised a lord to the purple so all were either promoted regardless of achievement or promoted to jobs in the corners of the castle close to the stables, where they were promptly forgotten. No lord was ever openly beheaded or demoted.

The king also decided to implement a program attempting to match the right vassals to the right jobs. He called it Universe, but the vassals called it The Lottery because the odds against a vassal playing and winning were astronomical. The lords did not like the program because it tied their hands, so they immediately set about subverting it. The program evolved into a process whereby the lords continued to make personnel moves just as they always had, but informed Universe afterwards. This made the lords happy. Universe then published the personnel moves that resulted from the efforts of Universe. This made the king happy. The name eventually was changed to a meaningless bureaucratic phrase, which at least reflected its real status.

As the lords grew in importance, so did the size of their staffs. The staffs in the castle outgrew its walls and outbuildings were produced or rented to house all the people and machines which were considered necessary. They produced nothing, but created enormous workloads on everyone. The vassals decided that "staffs" must be an acronym for "Special Taskers of All Foolish Fiefdom Silliness."

The stables were torn down to make room for the new castles. The animals died or were sold, and the manure supply dried up. There were no animals for plowing and food became scarce. The barbarians became aware of the weakness and the kingdom became less and less able to cope with their inroads. The king, finally understanding that the end was near unless he did something quickly, sent for new wise men, Fog and Smog. These men proved to be wiser than Smoke and Mirrors, and after a brief tour of the kingdom, quickly realized that the problem was that there were hardly any teeth left. All the energy of the stable was needed to maintain the ninety-nine percent of it that was now all tail, producing nothing, but consuming all.

The New Wise Men thereupon advised the king to behead all lords who had not enjoyed measurable success in the last two years. Doing as they advised, the king also wisely cut all staffs to ten percent of their former strength and reassigned the remainder to the care and feeding of animals. The animals and the vassals were moved into the castles and the remaining lords forced to move their offices to the stables. New lords were ennobled based on an objective evaluation of their demonstrated abilities to lead, organize and take risks...and nothing else. Soon everyone was doing what he was best at, they were happy and production rose sharply and quickly. The kingdom was saved.

The moral: Manager, heal thyself.
Subordinate Moral: He, who would have meetings, must be
prepared to meet himself.

Management is a full time endeavor. Keeping an
organization healthy demands the full and constant attention of the
manager. The nobles were not bad people, merely men thrust,
through ignorance, into positions for which they were not
prepared, and in many cases for which they had no aptitude or
interest. Full-time managers do not need large staffs because they
keep their own eyes and those of the work force steadily focused on
the main purpose for which the organization exists.

The management function is no more important than the
technical function and one should not exist without the other. The
lords forgot what it was like to be a vassal, then forgot about the
vassals altogether in their manic castle building. Managers must
spend the majority of their time supporting the work force, not
themselves. Management needs cannot be ignored, but they should
take second place to workplace needs.

Finally, managers should be chosen because they want to
help people and the organization function better, not because they
want to be nobles, or because they were good technicians. Good
technicians and good managers are often two different kinds of
people. The lords functioned exceptionally well as technicians.
Pick a manager because he or she has demonstrated management
aptitude, not just technical aptitude, and you will avoid the stable's

predicament of losing good vassals while simultaneously gaining bad lords.

The Parables of the Tail with No Teeth, Part II

Into the Teeth of the Tale

Once upon a time, a castle stood in the midst of fertile fields in the Land of Red Tape. It was a large castle and, because this was so, many people labored within its walls. The French had a name for the function these people performed. They called it *bureaucracy*, but because the king of the castle was not French, he referred only to his castle staff. Whatever the name, the effect was the same; the staff grew and grew, without any relationship to the actual needs of the castle. The peasants referred to the king's staff as "the plague," because there did not seem to be anyway to stop its spread.

Thomas à Bucket was a vassal on this staff. He was tall with long blond hair that seemed forever to fall over his eyes. He had keen gray eyes set above a straight nose and a wispy blond Vandyke beard. He was well muscled, which made him elegant to look upon regardless of his attire.

Thomas was new to the castle, having recently been brought in from the hinterlands where he had been in charge of marketing manure on the edges of the realm. He became factotum to Sir Lancelot, close to the king's chambers in the Power Tower. Sir Lancelot assigned him to be liaison with the stable.

Thomas quickly noticed that the castle could benefit by acquiring better manure handling tools used in neighboring realms. So it came to pass that he worked out the details of the acquisition and created a briefing to convince the Lords of the Conference Table to issue the needed amount of gold. This is the story of what happened to Thomas.

Thomas eventually briefed his plan to the Prince of the Piles in the Grand Hall of the Treasury. The reputation and opulence of the hall were intimidating (not to mention the reputation and opulence of the nobles who gathered there to hear him). Thomas remembered the rumors that a considerable part of the treasury had been used to decorate it, and them. He contrasted the scene in the Grand Hall with the conditions of the stables and experienced his first sinking feeling since arriving at the castle.

Thomas finished his briefing and stood expectantly before the round table leaning on the broadsword he had used as a pointer. Sir Lancelot had given it to him saying that no vassal of his was going to use one of those effeminate epees. "Besides who was going to argue with someone with a broadsword in his hands," the cagey knight had said with a wink.

Thomas was also pleased with his charts. A visiting Italian had painted them. *What was his name again . . . Angelo? Yes that was it: Michael Angelo.* Thomas most liked the chart that showed an arm thrust from a cloud toward the king, a state-of-the-art pitchfork hanging by its handle on the tip of the outstretched finger.

It was all worthwhile now. Thomas shifted his feet fitfully. *Even the long hours of acrimonious argument; the grueling fact-finding trip to several stables; the disappointments when other parts of the staff didn't respond with their contributions on time, if at all; and the several delays and cancellations of the decision briefing. Well, maybe those cancellations still rankle a bit. Then the frantic last minute preparations, lost sleep and stomach aches. All for naught mostly since a page brought the message, often at the last minute, that once again, the briefing would not take place as scheduled. No reason was ever given, of course. Most inconsiderate!*

Then there was the horrific day when the Moor, Ibn Ad Hoc, the Prince of the Piles' chief advisor, walked out mid-way through his first presentation. It was an awful start on the road to the Prince of the Piles and this day. Ad Hoc had berated him at length on the artwork on the first few charts (this was before Michael Angelo had operated on them) and refused to listen to the content of the presentation. The Moor still did not know what Thomas was recommending and, what's more, was now complaining because he didn't. It was, of course, someone else's fault.

Thomas fretted while the Prince of the Piles conferred with

his personal staff and the Lord of the Hoard. He could catch only a word or phrase here and there, but it seemed that the prince was asking for opinions from everyone. *Spreading out any future blame?* He could also hear that, although none of the prince's staff had ever seen the equipment Thomas was proposing to buy, and had never seen the operation the equipment would improve, they were acting as though they knew all about it. Even more amazing to Thomas, they were taking a decidedly negative stance. *Incredible! Was it only mean-spirited ignorance or reluctance to acknowledge a good idea not their own? Holy hatchet, now they were suggesting that the problem needed more study! As if the subject has not already been studied for what seems like forever, and by the best peasants available. Well, surely the Lord of the Hoard will see the wisdom of my recommendation. Surely he will understand that more study will only mean more delay and higher costs. Surely.*

Finally, the Prince of the Piles drew himself up and addressed Thomas for the first time since the briefing had begun. "Well, young man, that was a very interesting briefing," he said.

Uh Oh, I am in trouble now!

"Yes, very interesting." The Lord of the Hoard shifted uncomfortably in his chair at the head of the table. "Uh, well, of course, you, uh, know this is a very important project--one that has my full attention. Uh, what is its name again?"

"Project Quicksand, sir!" Thomas spat it out with the

military precision that he had heard the prince loved.

"Ah, of course, Quicksand," said the Lord of the Hoard, "a very unusual name . . . and hard for me to remember sometimes," he concluded lamely.

And I am beginning to think quite apropos. Thomas fought the urge to slump.

"Yes, Jonas," the prince prided himself on his ability to remember the names of all the vassals in his organization, "well done. You have obviously done some very useful initial work here. I believe that we need to consider it as we transition (the prince also loved to use nouns as verbs) to the formal study phase on this very important purchase. In fact, I want you to be the special advisor to the study group that Sir John here will lead from here in the Golden Tower."

The Prince of the Piles turned to the Lord of the Hoard and made a gesture that implied he had handed over the problem. He then quickly shoved back his heavy wood and leather minithrone and, gesturing to his aide, hurried from the room. He left in his wake a bustle of horse holders fumbling with their chairs, in various stages of trying to rise before the prince disappeared.

Thomas busied himself with gathering up his charts, pointer sword, and pride. He tried hard not to meet the eyes of anyone else in the room. In fact, Thomas was soon alone in the room, except for his master, Sir Lancelot, who was looking at him sympathetically.

"Welcome to the Tower of Power, Thomas,"

Lancelot said as he beckoned Thomas to follow him from the hall.

"I cannot understand it, Sir," Thomas said to his master's broad back. "I had all my maces in line, the decision was clear. The urgency of quick action was clear! How can he just turn away and leave things hanging like that?"

"Yes, you do not understand, Thomas," Lancelot said as he turned down the hall leading back to their office. He was still a large man reminding Thomas that he was the greatest knight the castle had ever seen on the field. "Not that I blame you," he added tactfully. He pulled a walnut from his purse and began shucking it gratefully. "A pox on those busy-body Anti-Wal-Nuts! I hate being able to grab only these quick nuts in the hallways. The next thing those court jesters will do is ban walnut eating in the halls, then I will really be in trouble!" Walnut eating was anathema to a majority within the castle. Although the citizens of the kingdom had engaged in the habit for centuries, recent "revelations" by sorcerers suggested that walnut eating caused the pox and, in fact, mere contact with the shells meant eventual doom. The acorn lobby, of course, was in the forefront of the campaign to obliterate walnut eating.

Thomas glanced at the trail of shells streaming after Sir Lancelot and at the "No Walnut Eating in This Hall" sign on the wall and walked a little faster.

"Look, Thomas, you must understand the situation. This project costs a lot of gold and is very controversial because the other towers fear for their own budgets. The king is the only one who is for it one hundred percent . . . and he is dying. Nobody knows what the new king will think about it. The prince relies on the advice of others such as the Lord of the Hoard, but that lord did not get where he is by making decisions that might anger a king. On the contrary, he got there by making no decisions at all. He never left his fingerprints on anything important, ever."

"But, I still do not understand, Sir Lancelot. I is he not paid to make decisions, to make sure the castle is prosperous?"

"What he is being paid to do and what the culture of the Knights of the Conference Table tells him he *must* do are two different things, I am afraid." Sir Lancelot stopped to ladle water out of one of the many buckets dotting the hallway. His long blond-gray locks and beard glistened from the stray drops. "The castle functions as well as it does because of vassals like you; castle servants who know what needs to be done. Then, you compound your error, because you are not politically attuned, by doing something right without regard to whether it will bother—or maybe *not* bother—a lord off in some corner of the castle somewhere.

"Nobles like the Lord of the Hoard have a lot more to worry about. He worked hard to get where he is. He had to compromise a lot in the process and now he thinks he owes it to

himself to hang on to what cost him so much to achieve. He knows
he is not well prepared for his position--the system is designed to
enhance privilege, not encourage altruism--and he has to protect
himself as best he can from criticism or the worst of all
eventualities, sacking, and loss of his self-esteem. He is just a
human being trying to get along in a hostile environment he did not
make and cannot change. He has to go along to get along."

They reached their chamber but Sir Lancelot hesitated to
enter. "I would like to go back to my cell but I really need another
walnut. Let us stand here in the hall a while. Besides, the scenery is
excellent, eh?" Sir Lancelot's eyes were following the undulations
of a lovely young serving wench receding down the hallway. "I
understand the king will soon proscribe the innocent pleasure of
wench-watching, too." He frowned.

"Yes, it is Castle Correctness," smiled Thomas. "Sir, what
you are saying sounds very cynical to me. Are you seriously telling
me that our nobles are more worried about themselves than they
are in serving the king?"

Sir Lancelot threw a mocking look at Thomas. "Well, that
is really only true in the exception but, I admit, it often looks that
way. You have heard the expression 'If it were not for bad
management, we would not have any at all.' have you not?"

Thomas nodded.

"In this most exalted castle," Sir Lancelot continued, "it
often seems like we do not have any at all. True, we have

management positions and lords in them. But, the actual process of castle management itself seems alien, even arcane, to many of us. Much of what our nobles claim to be management seems to many to be just the normal bureaucratic responses to stimuli. That is to say, what often happens is a reactive response, not programmed action resulting from long-range planning. The lord sits on the status quo until forced off by fiat or unforeseen circumstance."

Sir Lancelot finished his walnut, immediately reached into his purse . . . and discovered he had eaten his last one. Seeing the stricken look on Lancelot's face, Thomas motioned that they walk to the nearest walnut stand.

"An old lord once told me," Sir Lancelot said wearily, "in frustration, I think, over my badgering him to make a long overdue decision. He said that his philosophy was to make as few changes as possible in any tower he was in charge of. His goal was to do only enough to maintain the status quo. He did not want to exceed castle normalcy because that was too risky. On the other hand, he wanted to avoid obvious failure at any cost. His reward was the same, no matter what he did as long as it did not result in demonstrable failure. Even that might not matter, but one never knew for sure."

"I just cannot believe it, Sir! You mean to tell me that this man wanted to succeed by doing *nothing*!" Thomas had the sudden and unfamiliar desire to eat one of Sir Lancelot's walnuts.

"That is what I am saying, Thomas. He had been around a

long time and knew how the joust was played."

"But how does anything ever get done?" Thomas was incredulous. "If you do not try to improve, to make progress, do you not then eventually fall behind and fail anyway?"

"True, but that only affects those who are in charge when the day of reckoning finally comes. Our lords have figured that one out. They never stay in one place very long. They move on as fast as they can. That minimizes being in the wrong place at the wrong time. Anyway, responsibility is so diffused in the castle that it is rarely possible to point the finger of guilt at any specific lord. They can make decisions resulting in short term gains, regardless of long-term consequences.

"In truth, it is not all bad, Thomas. Look at it this way. The vassals, thereby, actually have a lot more power than the lords think they do. All you must do is figure out a way to get the job done that does not involve a lordly decision. You must, of course, be willing to put your own neck on the block. Adopt our cavalry's philosophy: consider a non-decision to be a yes decision and forge ahead until a noble actually says no. In this castle you receive very few no's . . . because that in itself is a decision and therefore a risk."

"Gadzooks, I do not know what to think right now. I feel like you just kicked me in the codpiece. Guess I am pretty naive, eh?" Thomas was looking at the floor, noticing nothing, lost in awful contemplation.

Sir Lancelot said, "Lords are smart and mostly are quite happy when something good happens for the castle. Surprised but happy." Sir Lancelot smiled. "In the same way that you insist that they try to understand you and your problems, so you should try to understand their world and how they must cope with it."

"But what do I do now? How do I cope with this new study group? Getting that equipment now is important for the stable. More delay could really hurt us and I cannot seem to convince the lords of that."

Sir Lancelot shrugged in resignation and led the way back to his office. He closed the door and they both sat.

"Look, Thomas," Sir Lancelot resumed, "I do not have *the* answer to your question. You will keep pushing and maybe you will compromise in the end. But do not give up and eventually you will find a way."

While Sir Lancelot was talking, he was also urgently searching through his desk for a bag of walnuts. With a look of elated triumph, he suddenly pulled an old, very crumpled, sack out of a drawer.

As he contentedly began his routine with the walnut, Sir Lancelot offered, "I guess you are thinking I am doing a good job of quadrilling around your question, but think about this: this castle is a unique management challenge. It is not only a bureaucracy but also a highly technical activity. Classic management philosophy as applied to our mercantile world is inadequate at best."

Sir Lancelot stopped again and started working on his tenth walnut since the briefing. "You know," he mused as he glanced at the partly unrolled parchment on his desk, "something like over ninety percent of all our vassals receive top performance evaluations every year. I do not remember exactly, but I think those receiving deficient judgements are less than one percent. My bet is that one reason for that is that you cannot get someone else to take the sluggards off your hands if you establish that kind of negative paper trail. So, instead, you give them a good assessment, and maybe a promotion, and increase your odds of passing the problem off to some other unsuspecting lord."

"Who is probably trying to do the same thing right back," Thomas interrupted.

"Right. Well, this is the realm in which we function." Sir Lancelot paused, shook himself in realization of his digression, and returned to the point. "You want a solution from me, do you not? Well, here is my tuppence worth. I believe that a process of renewal is needed and has to start from the top . . . with the recognition that there really is a problem and that the lords must take an active part in solving it. Not leave it up to the social reformers in the Ivory Tower who, as far as I am concerned, are part of the problem to begin with. Our nobility has to realize that not to move forward is to fall backwards."

"The status quo quickly becomes the status quo ante," Thomas said.

"Right again! We must declare that people, not machines, are the most important cogs in this cart's wheel . . . and treat them like people, not axles. We need to use care in hiring them, care in training them and a lot of care in promoting them. Finally, and this is very important, do not allow our people (and for Merlin's sake stop encouraging them) to move around the castle willy-nilly from tower to tower, without connection and no linearity of purpose."

Sir Lancelot snatched an Ivory Tower parchment broadside from atop his in-basket. He sighed and spoke again, almost to himself, "Stress management! Another presentation on stress management!" He slammed the paper into his chamber pot. "What I want to see is help in avoiding stress, not managing it! A concerted attempt to remove the causes of stress!"

Sir Lancelot looked up to see that Thomas was leaving. "Now that would be cause for optimism, would it not," he yelled at the closing door.

Outside, no closer to a resolution of his immediate problem, Thomas was deciding to buy his own sack of walnuts.

The moral: The decision to put off decision is in itself a decision—a universally bad one.

The castle management philosophy was to never put off until tomorrow what you can put off until the day after tomorrow. Inaction concerning the business is prohibitively costly. A questionable decision is usually better than no decision at all. Decisions in a bureaucracy rarely have the staying power of the Ten Commandments. Make the decision and be prepared to modify it later if necessary.

Personnel decisions are another kettle of worms. In a litigious workplace, the problem only gets worse as fear of lawsuit replaces fear of employee anger as the number one inhibitor of decision. Do what you think is right and document, document, document your actions. It is a knack that becomes best with plenty of practice.

The Parables of the Tail with No Teeth, Part III

The Tarnished Teeth of the Golden Tail

Once upon a time, a castle stood in the midst of fertile fields in the Land of Red Tape. The castle prospered greatly, and the number and size of its towers grew majestically. No tower, however, grew more than the Tower of Gold. The king added floor after floor to that tower to accommodate the steady, positive gold flow into the castle. The lords of the castle vied with one another to build higher towers but the Golden Tower, as it was commonly known (only yellow stone could be used in its construction), always towered over all the other towers.

The presence of so much gold acted as a magnet for ideas on how to trade the gold for goods and services the other towers wanted. As a defense against overzealous raids on the Golden Hoard, the Lord of the Hoard created a gauntlet of vassals trained by Bureaucraticus of Bloat, the castle's official Philosopher of Organization. These Goldkeepers had to be thwarted before receiving any gold.

The Lord of the Hoard had a very simple strategy. Each time gold spending increased; he added a new floor to his tower.

Then he created a new office that had to be traversed, with a new form in hand, when attempting to obtain any of the castle's gold.

At the time of our story the tower consisted of 21 floors, 21 hoops to leap through. This is the account of how our hero, Thomas à Bucket, stormed this bullionary bastion and its Goldkeepers.

Thomas, with Herculean effort, finally received permission to acquire the equipment with which he sought to modernize operations in the stables. The permission was, not uncommonly, less than clear. Actually, it came more in the form of the lack of a firm negative. Thomas followed the advice of his lord and mentor, Sir Lancelot, and simply kept moving forward absent any firm direction to the contrary. Eventually, he created that egregious bureaucratic anomaly, the *fait accompli*. *Accomplis* occurred because either no one understood a project but was disinclined to reveal the fact, or the cost of it was too low to break the attention threshold of the Goldkeepers.

Thomas was aware that he was in a race, a race that pitted his progress through the budgetary minefield against the acceleration of technological creativity. He had heard many tales of expensive purchases of equipment that were already relegated to the ash heap of progress by the time the equipment arrived in the castle.

This was particularly true of sophisticated scribe tools. Thomas was aware, for example, of the abacus, which had arrived from the East a few years before. At first, they were scarce and only lords were allowed to have them. Gradually the supply increased so that the abacus slowly trickled down to the vassals.

Furthermore, the castle lacked any semblance of configuration control. The vassals were always behind the technological power curve, never able to catch up. The lords and vassals of each tower acquired what they wanted, without regard to what the other towers were doing. Many even ignored what other parts of the same tower were doing. Thomas set out to avoid these problems in his acquisitions for the stables.

Thomas developed a teeth-to-tail concept for the stables. He wanted to modernize the feed handling and serving to the animals. He visualized a conveyor belt of leather stretched over wagon wheels upon which peasants shoveled food for the animals. The belt would run past the muzzles of the animals, which would be able to eat from it as the food on the belt passed by. Removal of the digestive results also would be by conveyor belt, although not by the same one (despite the strong suggestion of one Goldkeeper to do just that).

A marketing survey by the Tower of Tidings, announced by the Lord of the Crystal Ball, revealed that women were nine times as likely to put the manure on the fields of the realm. A minion in the Tower of Tidings convinced Lord Crystal Ball they should mix the manure with perfume. This did nothing for the quality of the manure but added to the allure of the otherwise mundane product, or so they claimed. The reality did not matter anyhow and Thomas was forced to add perfumed manure to his project description.

Thomas' first step was to begin the 25-5 process, a mainstay in the castles Fudget Cycle (the term the vassals used to refer to the budget). It was named 25-5 because twenty-five was the number of towers that had to affix their seals on the statement of work and five was the number of years that usually took.

Thomas' next step was to enter the Munificence Cycle by submitting his idea to the Tower's Fiscal Dreams of the Year package, the compendium off wish lists from all towers of the castle. The Dreams met reality first in the form of the Prince of the Piles' procedural guidance. This year the prince decided to list all Dreams in reverse alphabetical order. The year before they had been in alphabetical order, so this seemed to the prince to be a very sensible thing to do. Sadly, the immense effort to make this, his only, important decision of the year, forced him into a sickbed for a month.

The prince already had issued his planning guidance. Thomas was in luck; the prince had declared that year to be the "year of animal husbandry." His idea sailed through the Tower Program Development, Inter-Tower Castle Review, and Tower Re-review phases. His first setback occurred in the Ranking of the Dreams. His program was ranked behind a new suite for the Lord of the Flush in the Plumbing Tower. Nonetheless, it was ranked high enough to escape the budgetary axe and continued through the winnowing wallow.

The rankings received the Prince of the Piles' approval, and Thomas' tower submitted his program. Following the second Inter-Tower Review, the programs underwent the Prince's Review Group process. Again, his idea survived but by the time a third Inter-Tower Castle Review, and the Prince's Re-Review, took place, six months of the agony of constant rewrites (which changed the idea not a whit), began to take its toll on Thomas. He became very nervous, lost sleep, and began to imagine axe-bearing lords behind every column.

Finally, the Fiscal Dreams were submitted to the Tower of Gold, one of the toughest of the hoops. The Lord of the Hoard carried out a Forecast Review and a Fiscal Dreams Realization Plan was produced. Here the programs were assigned to different pots of gold located in the Tower of Gold (according to purpose and tower): Thomas' was assigned to the Rework and Diddle, or R&D, pot.

At this point, the entire package of Fiscal Dreams was subjected to the New Guidance from the Prince of the Piles' process. This was where the prince could change his mind, as he was often wont to do. As usual this process wreaked much havoc within the towers but again Thomas was lucky; his program survived, although changed a bit to specify cheaper materials: cow versus goat skin for the conveyor belts. Thomas was just happy someone had not specified horsehide.

Following the fourth Inter-Tower Castle Review, the costs of the Fiscal Dreams were submitted and suffered the second review by the Lord of the Hoard. Then, the Lord of the Hoard complained about a "wholesale and unjustified raid" on his precious pots of gold and ordered restraint during the fifth Inter-Tower Castle Review.

The results were submitted to the king who, much to the surprise and relief of Thomas, accepted his program—by now the many changes had brought his concept back almost to that with which he'd started (the perfume was still in it though). The king passed the Fiscal Dreams (many of which had turned to nightmares by this time) to the Lord of the Hoard with orders to hand over the requisite gold to the towers with surviving programs (the game winners). The Lord of the Hoard, unhappy but powerless at this point to change the plan any more, turned to the Lord of Debentures and his Tower of Debt to authorize the disbursement of the gold, and went into seclusion with a severe case of fiscal despair.

His share of the tower's pot of gold assured (so long as he spent it before the Lord of the Hoard changed his mind), Thomas set upon the third challenge of the budget contest. He entered the arcane world of procurement.

Thomas' first step was to fill out a Pot Raid (PR for short), a term the Lord of the Hoard had coined in a psychological attempt to keep usage of the pots of gold to a minimum. Thomas had never seen a PR so he went to the tower's Parchment Patrol to ask for advice.

Thomas entered the cell, which was actually a very opulent room, even by castle standards, proving that being a tail could be a pleasant experience. The desks and accoutrements were mahogany, the floor rug covered, the walls hung with the finest tapestries depicting axe-wielding Fugdeteers fending off the avaricious denizens of the towers, dressed as Vikings. He stood before the desk of one finely clad fop who was reading the betting sheet for Saturday's joust.

"Ah, yes. Umm, of course," a Parchment Patroller (peeper, for short) told him. "Uh, I am sure we can help you . . . I think. You must understand these things change regularly, so I must take care to give the right details."

Thomas nodded warily. He never trusted peepers, much less peeper dandies.

"Let us see," said the peeper, "we received the latest guidance just the other day." He pulled out a huge folder. "Yes, lets see, these are the changes we have received in the last month or so. The latest one should be in here. Ah, yes, here it is! Here you are, Master Thomas. You can use this guidance to fill out your PR."

"But I thought it was your job to fill these out. I have the information; you can worry about the format." Thomas began to back away.

"Well, yes, of course. Normally we would do that but we are a little short of hands right now, and have not the time." The peeper thrust the paper into Thomas' hand, and returned to his jousting-sheet.

Thomas returned to his desk, pulled out a large jar of ink and his strongest set of quills, the ones made from eagle feathers, and set to work. Two weeks later, having worn out enough quills to re-clothe a whole eagle, he thought he might be finished. He took the results of his labor back to the peeper.

"Ah, Master Thomas, you have returned . . . already." The peeper seemed amazed. "Uh, I see you have got your PR. But, what a shame! We have received six more changes to the format since you were here last. Here they are. Good Luck!"

Thomas grimaced in resignation and returned to this desk. Quick learner that he was, he decided not to risk a repeat of this problem. He stayed up all night and returned early the next morning. No one was there. A passerby explained that all the peepers were in class, learning the whole new format for PRs that was to be initiated the next day. Unfortunately, there would be no one available to take care of him this day, so he would have to wait until tomorrow . . . and the new format.

Thomas was not about to give up that easily. He took the PR directly to the Tower of Gold himself. Once there, he resorted to the Bureaucratic Fib Ploy. He told the minion Goldwatcher that the king had ordered the Prince of the Piles to see that this project was completed as soon as possible, if not sooner. He flashed his Power Tower pass and the Goldwatcher took the PR with trembling hands.

"Right away, sir, right away. Consider the task finished already. I will send for you immediately we are finished."

Thomas waited three weeks. During those weeks, no one would, or could, tell him the status of his PR. He waited impatiently with increasing frustration. Finally, one of his tower's peepers sent a page to Thomas with the PR and a note.

"Unfortunately," the note said in a tone that suggested the writer did not think it was really all that unfortunate, "Line Two has an error in it. It will have to be redone and, of course, resubmitted in the new format. Goldwatchers will not touch this." Thomas was a victim of the old Goldwatchers' Trickery Trick: tell them anything to get them out of face-to-face range. Even a prince could not buck this system.

Thomas sighed but got out a new jar of ink, and another bird's worth of quills, and set to work. Two days later, he returned to the peeper with the new PR in the new format. "Looks good to me," the peeper said while throwing into his out basket without a look. He dismissed Thomas with a "We will get right on this and let you know as soon as possible."

Thomas waited two more weeks before the page returned with the PR, and a note of apology. "Sorry it took so long but you see there was an error in Line Three. Please redo and resubmit as

soon as possible. Time is getting short you know." This continued
through Line 17, although the time spent on each line got shorter
each time. At Line 17 Thomas finally broke, and lost his temper.
He hastened to see his master and friend, Sir Lancelot.

Thomas burst into Sir Lancelot's office and stood, shaking,
before his mentor's desk. "What can it be, my boy? You seem very
excited. Here, have a walnut, sit down, and relax. Can it be all that
bad?" Lancelot retrieved his old and worn walnut bag from a
drawer and passed it over to Thomas.

The walnuts were now illicit since walnuts had been
banned from the castle by a king who did not like them and did not
think anyone else should either. Life in the castle was becoming
less pleasant all the time, as the self-proclaimed saviors of
everyone else grew stronger. Even drinking mead in the castle's
dining room was banned after an Elector had written
disapprovingly to the king.

"I want to call someone out for a joust, sir, but I think I
would have to take on the entire Golden Tower. It has taken more
than three months to get my PR done; it has now been sent back 17
times, one small error at a time, by seventeen different
Goldwatchers. I am angry and frustrated and beginning to wonder
if it is all worthwhile." Thomas took a walnut and began to calm
down.

"Ah, I see! You have been caught in the quite vicious
budgetary circle for the first time. This could be quite serious.

There is no cure for the Budgetary Blues."

"Please, do not jape me, sir; I am in no mood for it. What I need is help. How do I break out of this vicious circle?" Thomas had another walnut.

He began to get hold of himself. "What is going on? Do not these people realize that this is an important project, and they are going to destroy it with their silly rules? There are so many different levels that must affix their seals. Each one has different rules. No tower or floor in a tower, talks to any other tower or floor but each one refuses to put its seal on until everything meets its complete approval according to the latest rules, which change regularly and without notice. The next level then will not accept it because the parchmentwork does not agree with *their* latest rules."

"Well, you are partly right, Thomas." Lancelot said. "They are silly but I am not sure that any set of instructions that change as often as these do can be called rules. Besides, they do not exist to help the process but rather to give peepers and Goldwatchers something to do that makes them feel important. In many ways, they are the ones who run this castle, which is too bad, because they are also the ones least able to do so. They cannot understand what we are trying to do from their distant perspective. They only know parchmentwork and numbers. They can add and subtract, and use an abacus but they have no idea what is important and what is not. Consequently, the peepers can only watch the parchmentwork go by them and find unimportant things to complain about. They, and their process, have taken over the castle."

"Then it is out of control,"" exclaimed Thomas.

"Almost, Thomas, almost. The peepers and Goldwatchers have succeeded in making the whole process so complex, so hard to grasp and keep up with, that most lords quickly lose interest in trying to understand it. They turn away; let their vassals run it with little supervision. Even if you are successful enough to have a pot of gold assigned to your particular project, the rules force you to spend it irrationally. You can have a full pot there, but you cannot use it to refill your empty pot here. The rules they insist upon contribute to our unreasonably high costs, but they continue to claim that their only goal is to save gold. Remember the chamber pots that cost the castle 80 pieces of gold each?

"Heaven help you if you wait too long to spend your gold. Even if you have a good reason to hold it for a while, if a peeper finds your pot of gold, he can take your gold and give it to someone else without even asking you. They tell you how much you can have, for what, when you have to spend it, and they can change the rules and the size of the pots anytime they want to. So, yes, there is *control* in this castle, but it is in all the wrong hands."

Thomas' agitation was obviously returning as he had gotten up and was pacing Lancelot's office furiously. Finally, he asked, "So what can be done? Surely we cannot go on like this indefinitely. What is the answer?"

Sir Lancelot shifted on his stool and looked directly into Thomas' eyes. "It seems to me that the lords have to regain control over their own affairs. After all, we pay them a lot of gold. They have many perquisites. They are considered important people but they are not allowed to make important decisions. One important decision they ought to be able to make is how to spend their own gold to do the things in their towers for which they are responsible. Tear down the Golden Tower and give the pots to the lords."

Thomas recoiled in horror over the idea. It sounded to him like leaving the kettle only to fall into the fire.

Sir Lancelot jumped up from his chair. "And never, never give the service towers money of their own," he exclaimed. "It only allows them to operate programs of their own, which always take precedent over those of the towers they are supposed to be serving."

Thomas sat quietly, waiting for the storm to subside. He had heard it all before.

Sir Lancelot quickly scooped the walnut bag into its drawer as a scribe hurried in with the latest important parchmentwork for him to examine. If the scribe noticed the telltale remains in the shuckstray and on the desk, then he was bright enough not to show it.

"You know, there is another step we need to take," said Lancelot, scraping walnut husks from his desk into a leather cup. "I have been up to pushing a new idea: We should sort our manure into various grades. It is not a new idea but I think the time has come for it."

"It sounds great to me, too, sir," said young Thomas à Bucket, hoping his words contained more enthusiasm than did his mind, "so why do you not recommend it?"

"Well, I once succeeded in having a study initiated. One of the first actions was a conference to determine what the grades of manure would be." Sir Lancelot was now visibly exuding disgust. "The meeting was attended by representatives from the Towers of Gold and Tidings, the lords of the Abacus and of the Reap managed to come themselves. I even made certain that a manureologist was present.

"But no one could come from the stables. The staffs of the other towers did not believe the expertise of the stable was either necessary or useful since, in their minds, this was a financial question pure and simple. So they were not invited.

"Well, in keeping with the time honored ways of bureaucracy, the conferees first determined what they wanted to do and how they wanted to do it, then set about justifying the newly recognized outcome of the effort. This was easy; they merely wrote a new requirement to be satisfied by it.

"All they wanted to do was maximize profits. The wanted to grade the manure in three qualities: new improved, improved, and super blend. Being bureaucrats not constrained by the laws of economics, they also decided to grade in reverse of availability.

The most abundant was to be priced high so they could make the most money from it. This was called the new improved variety, which they figured would increase demand. Superblend was whatever happened to be left on the floor after normal collections were made. This was priced the next highest to create the illusion that it was the best, so they could get rid of it all. Improved was in the middle, that which would be used within the castle itself."

Sir Lancelot shifted stiffly in his chair, reached again for the much-abused walnut bag, sighed loudly, and then continued. "A committee was formed—it was called the Constipation Committee because it took so long to produce anything—to decide the best way to sell the manure directly. They discussed a manure market wherein the farmers could come every day to see the previous day's output and bid on the piles.

"But they had trouble settling on the size, mixture, and freshness of the piles. There were some who wished to charge more for the freshest regardless of quality, which, of course, was generally lower. Others claimed the older, maturer piles were worth more. There were even some who said that the castle should not provide fresh manure at all, that the farmers' own animals should be able to do it better. It went on like this until they finally gave up and dropped the whole idea."

Thomas decided it was time to leave. He needed cheering, not more discouragement. He waved goodbye to the glazed eyes of Sir Lancelot, hairy chin upon hands, contemplating what could have been "I will fight on," Thomas said, mostly to himself.

But, then he discovered another Vicious Circle. He needed to purchase extra parts that the vassal in the Tower of Plumbing and Stalling, who handled the acquisition for Thomas' project, failed to realize were necessary. This often happened--sometimes in epic proportions-- because project managers, like Thomas, were not allowed to control what or from whom, materials were acquired. Once the project was approved, someone totally removed from the sponsoring tower took over. One had to take what one got.

Unfortunately, they each cost less than 500 pieces of gold, and had to be paid for out of his tower's General Pot. Sadly, the General Pot was empty. He had gold left over in his own pot but could not spend it because of the General Pot Rule. He was not allowed to transfer his gold to the General Pot but had to wait until the Lord of the Stables decided to take it. Although the gold was in his pot (and he could even go to the Tower of Gold and see it there), he could not buy the articles he needed.

Finally, when the equipment arrived, he ran into The Bureaucratic Law of Non-Juxtaposition, which the peasants called the "you cannot get there from here" syndrome. He needed to make room for the new machinery by moving stalls in the stables. He was not allowed to do it himself, only peasants from the Tower of Plumbing and Stalling could do that. All the men of the Stalling Tower were busy renovating the Lord of the Flushes suite and were not available. Thomas was told that they would not be able to get to his project for many months, if ever.

Thomas gave up, compromised, and completed the project with half the efficiency he'd originally envisioned. Bureaucracy won, the castle lost. Again.

The moral: An oft-watched pot and too many cooks foil the broth.

A dynamic organization features empowered doers, imbued with shared goals, and fettered only by a group-common sense

The classic bureaucracy is replete with rules—rules that constrain and restrict, that channel human actions into foreseeable avenues. They are meant to protect but end up hobbling initiative and organizational goals.

The essence of a dynamic bureaucracy is the willingness to accept some mistakes (which are often not mistakes at all but simply another approach), suffer more messiness, while focussing on goals and success, not superfluous functions and unrealistic timelines.

While leadership must offer some control, that should take the form of guidance (unacceptable behavior—illegal, immoral, unethical), while leaving the positive, how-to, aspects to those as low on the totem pole as possible.

It is scary at first, much more effective—and fun—in the end.

The Parables of the Tail with No Teeth, Part IV

The Tale of the Tested Tooth and Tail

Once upon a time, a castle stood in the midst of fertile fields in the Land of Red Tape. It was a very large castle. Bureaucracy, which was always a threat to consume any of the castles of the Land of Red Tape, had built and then thoroughly engulfed this one. Laborers had been building the castle's expanding foundations with layer upon layer of parchmentwork.

These were not good times for the castle. A pestilence had wiped out a whole generation of vassals; leaving the castle peopled with mostly very young vassals and very old lords. The young vassals didn't respect the old lords, and believed these lords were no longer functional. The old lords doubted that the callow vassals could work as well as the lords did when they were young and tested in war. These deeply felt lordly beliefs, and the very foundations of the castle, were about to be tested.

Barbarians on the castle's southern frontier, the area served by the South stable, suddenly attacked the kingdom. These Barbarians were a particularly cunning and ferocious race of people from the edge of the world known as The Middle Muddle. Saddamn Ibn Sain, a small and mustachioed man, ruled them viciously and mercilessly. His diminutive size contrasted with his very large head, which unfortunately for the castle, was made up mostly of fat protecting a very large ego.

Saddamn was evil and cruel in full and equal measure; his capacity for jealousy and covetousness often overflowed. He loved to drench his greens in salad oil and, despite having plenty of salad oil seeds in his own lands, he wanted more; he wanted the seeds that the castle's peasants grew on the Land of Red Tape. They derived a pleasing sweet fluid from these seeds because of the distinctive manure that the stables produced for use on its exceptional plants.

Saddamn began his grab by sending small forays of horsemen into the castle's fields to bring back samples of the special salad oil seeds. This was the first of many mistakes he made during what became known as the Great Salad Oil War. It gave the king's martial knights, the Knights-Lanced, warning and time to prepare for war. They needed time and so did the castle's stables. Saddamn's second mistake was to believe that the castle suffered a manure shortage. On the contrary, this castle was awash in it. This was no time to diminish its customers.

The Knights-Lanced consisted of discrete components: those who rode horses were preeminent, those who could travel and fight only on foot were held in esteem as low as their physical location. Knights-Lanced who fought from ships were elitist and the other

Knights-Lanced disliked them intensely. There were other knights, including the Knights-Shocked, those who led every charge and carried out the most dangerous tasks of war. Thus, each kind of Knight planned and fought separately and, unless forced to do so by the king, did not cooperate any other kind of knight.

This situation also prevailed among the Knights-Errant, who separately served each kind of Knight. The knightly separateness meant that all Knights-Lanced and their Knights-Errant each believed they produced very unique manure. The Knights-Lanced wanted only their Knights-Errant to handle the manure. They believed only their own kind would do their bidding without the cavil of the civilian stables, but the Knights-Errant weren't as able to process manure as the well-established stables. Furthermore, all the Knights strove mightily if foolishly to be different from all the other Knights. Thereby, the processes of knightly accumulation of manure and distribution of manure became vastly incompatible.

The Knights-Lanced organized a military command post at the southern boundary of the Land of Red Tape, from which to repulse the Barbarians. The Joint Chiefs of the Knights picked the Lord of the Horde as commander of the expeditionary force. The Lord of the Horde, knowing the value of manure collection and removal to his endeavor, quickly created a Joint Uniformed Manure Baggers Liaison Element, or JUMBLE, to ensure expeditious disposal of all manure.

Into this critical situation strode our hero, Thomas à Bucket.

This is the story of how he and the castle fared during the Great Salad Oil War.

Thomas was the son of an earnest, therefore poor lord, who was a life-long friend of Sir Lancelot's. Lancelot had promised Thomas' father to be guardian and mentor of the son. The crafty Sir Lancelot often used Thomas as a surrogate for his surreptitious fight against the castle's bureaucracy. Thomas was tall and handsome, and possessed of pleasing voice and facile tongue. He took pride in his dress and was always neatly turned out. These traits alone would have been enough in this castle to help him get ahead but he also owned a clear, straightforward mind.

He was doing well in his career, thanks to Lancelot. Sir Lancelot, Senior Knight Emeritus, had manipulated castle incompetence to become an important lord despite a pronounced streak of renegade in his character. He was also a consummate bureaucratic jockey. What success Lancelot and Thomas created together—the little they could expect against the glacier strength of bureaucracy—could be measured by the growing degree to which both were viewed with increasing suspicion and bafflement by the other denizens of the castle.

Sir Lancelot had recently sent Thomas off to the front to investigate how the JUMBLE was doing. Upon his return, Thomas rapped hard on the door of Lancelot's huge cubicle. The resounding crack of walnut shells under pressure often prevented the good lord from hearing sounds beyond the cavernous chamber. Sir Lancelot would try to throw the shells into his chamber pot--only the most important lords could have them in their chambers--but more often missed than hit the elusive receptacle.

"Come in, come in, whoever you may be," shouted Sir Lancelot, quickly moving the chamber pot out of the way of the swinging door. "Ah, my good vassal, 'tis you," he exclaimed in delight. "I have not seen you in a long while. How was your trip to investigate the JUMBLE, my son?"

Thomas gingerly entered, threading his way across the walnut shell strewn stone floor. He glanced at the chamber pot and chose a seat at some distance from it. "Not good, sir, not good."

"What happened, my boy?" Lancelot began the interrogation.

"It was a mess. Manure everywhere but no one knew how to disburse it. All kinds of excrement jumbled about in the JUMBLE. It was a *knightmare* (although not the fault of knight's mares) but I got it straightened out. So here I am, and glad to be back."

"And how did you succeed?" asked Lancelot with wonder in his voice.

"It was simple actually." Thomas pulled his chair closer to Lancelot's parchmentwork and walnut shell strewn desk. "I set up a farmer's market where the manure could be received, sorted and made available to buyers no matter the kind of agrarianist they were. They could easily pick up what they wanted when they wanted it. Remember the conveyor belt I invented to feed animals, and then carry away the inevitable results to the shipping area? Well, I just reversed the process: shipped, conveyed, sorted and stored in marked bins. Sort of one-stop shopping with all-knight service." "Well done, Thomas," laughed Lancelot. He rose from his chair, cleaned a corner of his desk and, perching in the vacated spot, continued seriously, "Now I want to see if you can do it again." As usual when Sir Lancelot wanted Thomas to do some dirty work for him, he was very solicitous. "Are you well rested now? Feeling hale?"

Thomas groaned. "Yes, I guess so," he replied quizzically. *What I really need is at least a fortnight of continuous sleep.*

"We are preparing the counter attack on Saddamn Ibn Sain and his Barbarians," said Lancelot without further preamble.

"That man lives up to his name. He is well and truly *insane*," Thomas remarked.

"Yes, I understand that is his nickname. Apt, but the prince has charged me with readying our manureological support to the Knights-Lanced. It will not be easy because each tower, each floor of every tower, each stable and each stall of every stable, has already built its own Watcher Tower from which to 'control' everything."

"What can they all possibly be watching—much less controlling?"

"Each other, Thomas, mostly each other. And they create new positions in each Watcher Tower almost daily. Each to watch the position invented just before. Thus the fat of bureaucracy encases the castle and each Watcher Tower in turn."

"Thus giving each lord a piece of the action and glory,"

interjected Thomas. "Yes, I know all about it. It was a problem I could not fix for the JUMBLE. We never knew what Watcher Tower to talk to in the castle--they changed almost daily. And when we did find someone, the answers given to our questions about deliveries were different from those given by the last Watcher Tower we talked to. The JUMBLErs quickly learned who gave what answers and to 'target' just the right Watcher Tower to get just the answer they wanted to receive."

Lancelot nodded vigorously. "We are dealing with rank amateurs here in the castle, Thomas. And, not only are they neophytes in manure production but war, but they will not admit any of it, ask for help, or cooperate with each other for fear of giving a rival an advantage on the Lords' Ladder."

"Nothing very new there," commented Thomas.

"True, but did you know that the Lords ignored a pact they had made only a month before? It was to use the Peeper Tower only in just such a case as this. It was forgotten in the scramble for glory. Deferring to the Peepers would mean giving up their chance for a place in the Castle Hall of Fame." Lancelot peered at Thomas ruefully.

"Well, obviously we may need more than one Watcher Tower involved but certainly less than a hundred. The Knights-Lanced need to know who is in charge. We can accomplish that by using only one Peeper Tower in our dealings with the JUMBLErs."

"Agreed, Thomas," sighed Lancelot, "but the King likes

many competing and insipid Watcher Towers because then *he* can be the only one in charge . . . the bureaucratic dissonance being much too thick to penetrate from below."

"Everyone in charge, thus no one in charge," Thomas grimaced, "We have seen it before, sir."

"Yes, Thomas, there is no central focus, rather a diffusion of authority. No castle can last long under those circumstances, and we owe our Knights better than that. So, you and I are going to try to change the situation and do so quickly."

Lancelot looked at Thomas earnestly, "I want you to inspect our stables and their preparations and make recommendations to me about what can be done to make them ready for the counterattack against Saddamn. But hurry, Thomas, hurry."

Thomas wasted little time going to visit what was supposed to be the principal watchtower of the castle, the Peeper Tower. He went straight to the cubicle of the Chief Peeper on duty then, Master Minder. Master Minder was behind his table looking out the window with a telescope.

"Cannot have too many peepers, especially in times like these," he said looking embarrassed as he swiftly hid the telescope from sight. His table was clean, his waste receptacle empty; it looked like Master Minder was not very busy.

"Thank you for seeing me. I know you must be very busy." Thomas looked around dubiously as he pulled up a stool in front of Minder. Faint, undulating groan-like sounds seeped into the room from beyond the door behind Master Minder.

"Well, to tell you the truth, I have been busier. I have been busier on a Sunday during Christmastide." Master Minder looked at the closed door, hesitated, then appeared to make a decision, "The whole truth is that I—we, have absolutely nothing to do."

In the face of Thomas' look of incredulity, Master Minder continued, "With all the new watchers towers helping the JUMBLE be rid of its manure, there is not much left for us to delve into. Most of it goes through the South Stable instead of us and . . . well, you can see the result." Minder threw open the door to the Peeper Center. The multiplied sounds of industrious snoring filled the room. "The Peeper Center usually is like that only in the wee hours of the morning," he expelled, as he propelled the door shut again.

"The prince, under pressure from the King and probably from the Lord of the South Stable, simply reacted thoughtlessly. Instead of consulting his usual advisors and using the operations and procedures that already existed--had been tested and worked--he abandoned them to embrace the perilous advice of Ibn Ad Hoc, his Moorish golf partner. We Peepers have dubbed everything that followed the Ad Hoc Approach." Master Minder looked furiously disgusted.

Sir Lancelot would call that `undervaluing good management practices. Thomas asked, "Are you saying that all plans, all procedures, all previous experience and the experienced, were just ignored?"

"Yes," exclaimed Minder as he crashed his fist onto the table, "that is exactly what I mean." He slumped back into his chair and visibly calming again, began to yawn. "Well, I have to go back on duty now, Master Thomas, so if you will excuse me . . . the plans were hard to find anyway, everything is lost in the Tower of Plans and Bans these days . . ." the last words trailed off into barely audible eddies of sound. Minder laid his head in his arms crossed on the table. Almost instantly his snores joined the chorus from behind the Peeper Center door.

Thomas shrugged, put away his notebook and folding quill with its portable inkwell, and quietly let himself out of the room.

Thomas next visited the South Stable. Those buildings were located on a high bluff not far from the Tower of Power. An aide to the Lord of the South Stable met him as soon as he arrived. The aide obviously wanted to control what Thomas saw and to whom he talked.

Thomas quickly noticed that, despite the vassals looking and dressing like those in other parts of the castle, they did not act or seem to think the same. The difference was most pronounced in the attitude toward the customers of their manure.

"Who are our customers?" asked Thomas of a supervising vassal he'd just met named Clod of Clyde.

"Customers?" The vassal looked suspiciously at Thomas, "I do not know and I do not care. What difference does it make anyway? We just produce what we want to and shovel it out the door. What anyone does with it after that is their problem, not mine."

Clod slammed his right fist into his left palm. "Look, the knights produce much manure, endless manure. Our job is to liberate them from it. Keep the storage piles small, so the odor does not reach the Power Tower."

"Um, yes, of course," responded a suddenly nervous Thomas. *And I did not believe it when Sir Lancelot told me what it was like here*. He tried again, "But surely you must know what they want, when they want it, and how they want it, eh?"

"Oh yes, of course," replied Clod, "I receive the TESTs from our Special Taskers of All Foolish Fiefdom Silliness . . . but I never look at them. Probably could not find them. Silly anyway. Filed by our staff in the Deep Cave. When what they want is different from what we want to give them, they do not get it anyway. So, you see, it really does not matter what they put in the TESTs."

"What are TESTs?"

"Total Empire Specification Tables, of course," Clod of Clyde looked even more suspiciously at Thomas, "say, where have you been all your life, young man?" Clod turned to leave in disgust.

"I knew that, just checking you," croaked Thomas to cover his embarrassment. He hadn't heard the term since his initial castle orientation. "But, but," he called after Clod, "what is the point of the TESTs then?"

"Look," spat Clod over his shoulder, "it is not my fault that the agrarianists don't always want what we are willing to give them. That's their problem, not mine."

"But maybe you do not understand their needs," called Thomas to the rapidly disappearing Clod of Clyde. *No maybe about it.*

Clod stopped, turned around, and yelled, "Look, it does not matter, I tell you. They chiefly want our best manure. And plenty of it. I ask you, if we gave *that* to them, the manure from the special animals we keep in the back stalls, then what? All the agrarianists would find out about it and want it. Soon our foes would find about it and steal our special animals. Loose lips sink manure!"

"But what good does the manure do if the agrarianists cannot use it?"

"Still it is not my problem. Go ask the Lord of the South Stable."

Thomas turned in disgust. *Fat chance of that.* He stalked off to the next bank of stalls. There he met Arno the Lame, who was in charge of quick manure deliveries for the South Stable.

Arno greeted Thomas cheerfully enough, "Direct to the front from the rear still warm! That is our motto. Welcome, my good lad."

Grinning, Thomas shook hands with Arno. As he did so he noticed several vassals he knew to be workers from the North and East stables. "I see you are using loaned-in vassals. How are they doing, Arno?"

"Oh, pretty good actually . . . after we train them in the ways of the South stable," replied Arno, "it is difficult since they come here thinking they know better than we. We have to convince them that we do not want their ideas, just their hands and backs."

Thomas looking around the stall, asked, "Where are your usual vassals from the South Stable, all I see are those from other stables?"

"Ah, they are on holiday," Arno looked sheepish. "We did not want to taint our valuable talent by contact with these new, *foreign,* vassals who simply do not understand our much better way of packaging manure."

"Um, yes, I see, but surely it is useful to have at least some experienced South Stablers here?"

"Not really," said Arno, "we have consistently refused to allow experienced South Stablers to work here—anyone with experience for that matter; we do not care how much they beg us. Their experience in other stalls of the South Stable is not relevant to us. Besides, we are saving them to take care of other stalls not involved in the war with Saddamn."

"How much experience have you and your staff had in supporting the Knights-Lanced during war?"

"None, absolutely none. That is the beauty of it, we can proceed without any of the preconceived notions the others would have brought to this effort." Arno smirked.

Thomas left without saying goodbye. *Who the gods would destroy, they first make ignorant.*

On the way out Thomas met a vassal, Ellen the Fair, he knew from the East Stable. While shaking her hand Thomas asked quickly under his breath, "How do you stand it here?"

"Oh, it is not so bad. Take that one for instance," she said pointing at Arno, "he only thinks he knows what is happening here, but when he gives us his plans, we quickly see that they are totally unworkable and go ahead and do things in the East Stable way. Our way works so much better than his, which I think he must see but cannot admit. Anyway, he does not, does not dare, change anything. He just proceeds to take credit for any ideas that work. Everyone is happy that way." Ellen paused, then looked into Thomas' eyes. "Worse, much worse, is the stress we have here, most of it lords induced."

"How is this so?" asked a suddenly alert Thomas.

"The lords have decreed that we must fill our slow nights with stress related courses devised by the Wise Men. One is *bi-cultural stress*; a course designed to induce stress all by itself. It is mostly for the new vassals from other towers and it encourages two diametrically opposed processes: assimilation into the South Stable's culture (although exactly why anyone would want to is beyond me), and how a vassal can simultaneously maintain his identity (which is also ridiculous since most want exactly to change their identities, into that of a lord). Obviously, this course is a major source of candidates for the *stress management workshop*."

"Stress Management! What a meaningless phrase!" Thomas grimaced.

"Right," Ellen said, "The vassals have big problems with

this one. They wonder why anyone would ever want to *manage* stress. They believed it was better simply to avoid it." "*Stress avoidance*," Thomas said, "now that has a ring to it. Of course, the Wise Men never ask the question of why there is stress in the castle in the first place. *Stress identification* would also be useful."

"That, my dear Thomas, "is anathema to the lords in this tower."

"All towers," interrupted Thomas.

Ellen nodded and continued. "The Wise Men, but probably not the lords, likely have a good idea what really causes the stress here, but of course have no interest in calling attention to *that*. Instead, the vassals were expected to bend to fit the bureaucracy and if they do not, well then, they can always go back to the village and starve."

"Some vassals could leave the castle," Thomas said, "but many don't because they refused to be beaten down and would not let the lords save the pot of gold they would have to give them when they retire."

"Right," said Ellen, "most vassals intended to get as much of that gold as possible, and look forward to that alluring conclusion to their association with the castle."

Thomas nodded his head knowingly and smiling to himself, he returned to the Tower of Power to seek out Sir Lancelot.

"Well, I have met the enemy and he is us," Thomas said as he strode into Sir Lancelot's chamber. "As the great philosopher,

Bureaucraticus of Bloat, once said, 'If Horizontal Layering is the rock, then Lack of Corporateness is the hard place.'"

"That bad, eh?"

"Worse. Every staff in the castle wants a piece of the action but all they can think of to do, is make sure that they must be consulted on every action, every decision. They have placed themselves in the central place of glory but only slow down everything. They add little of value to the effort."

"Well then, have you also met the answer?"

"Well, for one thing, we need training in crisis management for everyone in the castle."

"A crisis being defined, of course, as any time a lord is forced to make a decision?"

Thomas laughed. "Yes, sir!" Thomas was now excited, as he always was when allowed to describe his ideas. "But much more than that, we need to build a new, Super Peeper Tower, bigger and much more comfortable than what we have now."

"And beholden only to the prince and not all the lords?"

"Right, sir, and when we do not have a war, we can use it to practice war. We can make room in it for the prince, and even the King, to sit and meddle, er, I mean, lead. It would be a place where the vassals could learn to smell wars coming."

Thomas waved in the direction of the old Peeper Tower, "We should stock the Super Peeper Tower with the best of everything: stools, tables, and the best abacuses (all of one kind, of course). Soon all the best vassals would be working there, and the other watch towers will crumble in neglect."

"Very good, Thomas, I like it," Lancelot said with enthusiasm, "I will talk to the prince right away."

In the end, the Knights-Lanced repulsed the Barbarians. The prince set up a Super Peeper Tower, but gave it to the Lord of the South Stable, and the vassals working there did a splendid job while the lords continued to dither. The Knights-Lanced were successful in part because of the help of these vassals. The stable helped the castle to victory, not because of the way it was organized or led, but because of talented vassals concentrating only on the job at hand. The vassals ignored politics and bureaucracy and personal fortune to concentrate single-mindedly only on the war with Saddamn Ibn Sain.

Finally, after a lengthy period of argument, the lords decided to award pieces of gold to everyone who spent even one minute working--or in some cases just thinking about--the war. They gave the same number of coins from the Tower of Gold to every one of certain common endeavors, whatever the quality of their work. The lords of course received many more pieces than any of the vassals, to whom the credit should have gone. Thus, no vassal was entirely happy; the only point upon which they could agree was that the lords did not deserve the gold coins they had received.

It was not long before everything was restored to normal. The lords allowed the Super Peeper Tower of the South Stable to deteriorate into ruin. The next war approached unPeepered.

EPILOGUE

The king ordered that the usual Transitory Comprehensions be identified as lessons to learn, as they always were after large efforts such as the Great Salad Oil War. The prince transferred the onus to Sir Lancelot and Lancelot transferred it to Thomas à Bucket saying, "The result of skill or luck is often identical but, with luck, maybe you can show us the difference."

Thomas once again advanced the idea of a Super Peeper Tower, calling it the New Super Peeper Tower to distinguish it from the one being allowed to molder. It would be responsible for all war support by the stables. The king rejected the idea this time—just like the prince, he liked being able to visit the many centers of Ibn Ad Hoc to pretend that he was in charge. Since the war had been won, he found it easy to forget the chaos that had reigned along with him. When asked about it he would exclaim that the New Super Peeper Tower was too expensive, a waste of space. The Transitory Comprehensions learned during the war were codified, approved, then assigned and reassigned to lower and lower levels of the castle for rectification, while the lords eventually forgot them altogether. The chances were not very good that the castle would be any more ready for the next crisis. But at least the next time they could save the expense of drawing up new lessons; they could simply brush off the old ones.

The king, unhappy with Thomas' finding, aptly commissioned Lord Flush of the Tower of Plumbing and Stalling to finish the work. Lord Flush, after talking to all the lords of the castle, submitted the following *Lordly Crises Transitory Comprehensions* to the king.

1. **Do not** make a decision; it will come as a surprise to the vassals and cause disaster if one of them actually implements it out of consternation.

2. **Do not** take any responsibility; you might have to make a decision.

3. **Do** pile on as many layers of lords as possible; in case one makes a decision by mistake, no one will know who did it.

4. **Do** change policies often and drastically; this will confuse your critics and protect you from specific blame.

5. **Do not** plan; any plans in existence will quickly be scrapped in favor of an ad hoc operation fitting the personality of the lord in charge.

6. **Do not** volunteer; you likely will find yourself working in a Watcher Tower instead of another lord, who will join a staff and be awarded more gold because of his better visibility to the King and his princes.

7. **Do** change tower names and locations regularly; this will keep the workload to a manageable level.

8. **Do** not give anything to the vassals you send to other towers, they are in the company of enemies and no longer trustworthy.

9. **Do not** put experience and knowledge in control; they will only confuse and distress you.

10. **Do not** do Transitory Comprehensions, unless you love reruns.

The moral: Is this Crisis Management or management crisis?

The stables lacked the essential ingredients for good crisis management--predetermined procedures, universally agreed upon, commonly understood, and enforced. A clearly defined structure and accountability functioning in a fully equipped center for operations, manned by experienced or at least fully trained management and work force.

The king made the mistake--common among kings--of expecting common, complete and absolute fealty from his subjects. What he ran into were factions competing against each other and unwilling to share or cooperate as fully as the king expected. The king alone could not meet the overriding need for central crisis management. Constant and consistent supervision could only be given by focused lordship at the stable level.

The typical human mind boggles in contemplation of difficult, often expensive, decisions prompted by mere possibilities. The resultant planning, if any, is heavily pockmarked with holes, like buggy computer software. The holes are then filled with reactive, too quick and ad hoc decisions, which are more palliative than curative. The organization starts out behind and has a devil of a time catching up.

They, who would make crises manageable, must first plan and then be disciplined in executing the plan. Digression from this approach, in the extent of the deviation, will cause as much chaos and failure. Planning, especially long-range planning, is an unnatural act in our American culture. But we must try because, if we fail to plan, then we should at least prepare for failure.

The Parables of the Tail with No Teeth, Part V

The Tale of the Rearranged Tooth and Tail - Reformation

Once upon a time, a castle stood in the midst of fertile fields in the Land of Red Tape. Its verdant fields yielded fruitful fodder that fed plump animals that produced manure that was the castle's main source of gold. The castle was very rich in manure and gold, and its lords spent both very inefficiently. The lords of the castle didn't worry about how they dispersed the wealth of the castle because there was so much of it, particularly manure.

Agrarianites far and wide richly supported the castle in a royal manner, which equally richly befitted its rulers' inclinations. The procedure of production was prosaic but the manure did seem to work better than that from other castles, so the agrarianites were willing to give up more gold to use it.

That is, they were willing until the market changed. Some of the best customers changed their habits. New kings were beginning their reigns on nearby lands and imposing new gastronomic tastes on their subjects. The peasants, to whom the castle sold manure, found it necessary to change the crops they grew. They soon discovered that the castle's manure was not as effective for the new crops. Farms began to turn to other castles whose manure worked better.

New crops required new farming techniques. It was clear to many in the stables (though not to the lords) that the castle had to adopt new techniques in manure processing. The old "get it out the stable door as fast as possible no matter what the quality" way of doing business no longer worked. The old adage: "manure received quickly is still manure," was never more pertinent. The lords not only needed new processes but also needed new animals to generate different, higher quality manure.

Then came the pestilence. Crops died in the fields, fodder became scarce and was of poor quality. Gold also became scarce in the castle and spending had to be cut back. The lords were reluctant to change their spending habits and refused to admit that the problem existed. They continued to build new towers, though that meant less gold with which to fill the towers with useful objects. Only when the Lord of the Hoard took the lords to the treasury room and showed them all the empty gold pots, did they finally seriously address the castle's gold deficit.

The king and his Knights of the Conference Table had developed a consensus approach to administering the castle. They did nothing important, or painful, without complete unanimity. Despite desultory attempts at bonding the lords, they remained individuals who seldom completely agreed to any decision of import. Essential decisions became rare and individual lords rarely decided anything. When forced, they first tried to hide under a collegial conclusion, but if they couldn't smoke out other lords, then they merely allowed events to settle outcomes passively.

Thus it was that lordly-level decision making ground to a progress-retardant halt. The king and his Knights of the Conference Table formed hundreds of study groups to decide what to do. Soon it seemed like everyone was studying the problems of the castle, instead of producing manure, but no one was *solving* them. This then was the predicament into which our hero, Thomas à Bucket, was thrust one otherwise very fine day.

Sir Lancelot, Thomas' friend and mentor, beckoned him to the Tower of Power, where the king and the Conference Table lords kept their chambers. "Welcome Master Thomas," roared Sir Lancelot, as he heaved up from his seat scattering walnut shells all about him. Lancelot was a large, athletic man with long, graying hair and a full beard from which walnut shells were likely to fly when shaken.

Lancelot led Thomas over to the overstuffed pallet in the corner. "Sit, sit, make yourself comfortable, my lad," said Lancelot unctuously.

Too unctuously for Thomas' taste. *Uh oh, he wants me to do some more of his dirty work,* he thought as he brushed aside the strewn shells and sat as close to the edge as he could.

Lancelot quickly sat closely beside Thomas in a cacophony of crunching walnut shells. "Thomas, my boy, how good to see you. How have you been? It has been many a day since you have graced my humble chamber. How, pray tell, have you been?"

Thomas, feeling Lancelot's hot, walnut flavored breath upon his cheek, shrugged and gave in. "Not so well, sir, it is very hard on us in the stables right now. The peasants are disappearing, the vassals looking for work in other castles. Everywhere we look there are problems that we cannot solve without help from the lords, which of course is as rare as chamber pots in the latrines these days. The gold crisis is causing the stables to die the death of a thousand cuts. The Tower of Hearsay is working overtime cranking out new rumors. Morale is at an all-time low."

"The wise men have come up with another wonderful rubric," answered Lancelot, "'Tis called 'perception management'. You have to understand that lords do not understand low morale. They have either not experienced its causes or they have forgotten what it was like to be a vassal. Those who rose from the bottom began their careers during times when the castle had few denizens and most of those worked in the stables. Take the horse-parking problem, for instance. They did not have to worry about it then and, of course, since they have their own horse stalls now, they still do not have to worry. They just do not have any empathy with problems like those caused by the famous decision to have a small horse-parking lot. Since it was farther from the castle than the large horse lots, many parked their small horses in the large horse lots. People arriving later with large horses had to park in the small horse lot where their saddles were dented from the restless horses in the small spaces. It did not work out and the Lord of the Hitch had to call the whole thing off. Now they are trumpeting horse pooling as the answer, another thing *they* do not have to worry about, since they do not have to arrive before matins to find a space within walking distance of the castle."

"You are absolutely right, Sir, too many such 'little' things add up to big morale problems," exclaimed Thomas.

"Yes, my son," said Lancelot, patting Thomas on the shoulder, "but complaints do not solve our problems. You know how it is around here. We lords simply cannot agree on what to do, so nothing is done." Lancelot smiled and, looking Thomas directly in the eyes, said very slowly and distinctly, "But now, you Master Thomas, have a chance to do something about it."

Now Sir Lancelot laughed. "Oh, ho, you think I am going to ask you to do some more dirty work for me, do you not? I am shocked and devastated that you could think so ill of me." Lancelot turned away a moment, then looked back with a sly smile upon his face, "but, of course, you are right."

Thomas winced but said nothing. He loved this old warhorse that would not give up, and could not bear to disappoint him.

Suddenly looking serious, Lancelot began to explain. "Thomas, the Prince of the Piles wants to save us from an almost certain catastrophe if we do not do something soon. Bureaucraticus of Bloat recommended that he form an extraordinary cohort to be made up exclusively of vassals who can still think and act and look ahead. Vassals who have much experience . . . and the willingness to apply it for the good of castle. We even have a name for it: the Special Advisory Vassal Element, or SAVE for short. Is that not wonderful?" Lancelot looked at Thomas for agreement. Finding none immediately obvious, he hurried on.

"Thomas, I want you to lead this cohort. You have a head on your shoulders, you care, and you are not afraid to twiddle twaddling lords. You are young and inexperienced but I can help you with that minor difficulty. In short, I want you to be my envoy to this cohort. It will last only a short time. In return, I promise you an elevation and position here close to me. What do you say, my boy," Lancelot looked up. "Or do you want time to think?"

Thomas' mind was racing. *What an opportunity! What a risk! It is a chance to prove myself and it is a chance to destroy myself. It is a chance to advance all the ideas I have had and stop all the nonsense I have complained about so much.* He shifted his position to rid his rump of an intrusive shell he'd missed. *On the other hand, it is a chance to increase my frustration level also.* And then he decided, impulsively, compulsively, the only way he could.

"Of course I will, Sir. But then, you knew that did you not? I have tried too hard to make a difference, to improve things in the stables, to deny this opportunity . . . however dangerous it might be to me personally."

"Yes, I knew that, Thomas." Lancelot got up and began to pace the floor as anxiety drained from his heart. "With your help, my boy, I am going to make a difference, too."

So it was that Thomas found himself leading vassals chosen from the four stables of the Tower of Feculence. Each stable had its own lord, its own stables, and its own way of producing manure. The East Stable--each had an unimaginative, though geographically accurate, name--specialized in putting out large piles of semi-processed dung without regard to the needs expressed by the peasants. The South Stable put out some highly processed and much hardly-processed manure according to what the peasant said he wanted, not necessarily what he needed. The West Stable delivered small piles of highly processed excrement (almost to the point of sterility) to peasants who were happy to get anything they could have from the castle. The North Stable had to serve many different peasants so, not surprisingly; it assembled the most versatile manure.

The East Stable sent Master Gather, a crack rear end collections expert. The South Stable sent Mistress Win, who specialized in the processing of manure, Manureology. The West Stable provided a production line artist, Mistress McMethod. Because of its multipurpose manure manufacture, the North Stable sent a generalist, Master Ironbottom.

The Prince of the Piles also commanded the Lord of the Hoard and Lord of the Reap to send a vassal each. Or so the prince said. Rumor had it that those lords forced the prince to take their spies on the process. In the castle knowledge was indeed power and the lords of the Hoard and Reap above all else desire power. Thomas was forced to welcome Master Cuthbert Cutpurse from the Tower of Gold and Hal the Heedless from Tower of Collections.

Thomas himself added Arch of Texture, from the Tower of Plans and Bans, because Arch was an old friend, trustworthy and a seasoned planner. While planning was a frustrating experience in the castle, Arch possessed the equanimity required to survive.

One of Lord Bellicose's henchmen, Lord Peek, tried to send his own spy, Gilles of Gumshoe, but Thomas had had enough and put a large padlock on the SAVE door and gave keys only to those he trusted.

Presiding over the whole group was their "mother hen," Mistress Lorelei, their secretary. Hal of Heedless, who had once served in the king's navy, dubbed her SAVESEC. She was young but with strong motherly instincts, pulchritudinous, and handy with a quill. Thomas knew he was lucky to have pried this jewel out of the Lord of the Rod's maiden stable.

In their first meeting together, in a dank dungeon far from the Tower of Power (assigned to them by the Lord of the Whip with profuse but adamant apologies), Thomas gave the SAVEiors his (and Lancelot's) philosophy on princes and lords. "The lords," he said, "derive their power from the legitimacy that comes from being aristocrats. That power must be used wisely or it is lost. Just ask

King Edward the Late. As a class, our lords stopped leading, suffer from failing *vision*, and cannot agree among themselves on anything that is important. We suffer mightily the pain of bureaucratic gridlock. Our job is to help them regain competence so the castle can move forward again."

"Furthermore," said Thomas, gesturing recklessly with his arms as the other vassals edged their stools out of range, "their legitimacy was a matter of perceptions--the perceptions of the vassals and peasants. The lords must balance their power, through mutual concern and respect, with that of those they rule."

"Yes, I know what you mean," exclaimed Mistress Win, "we are different from the inhabitants of the castle when the lords were young. But not in the way they think. I have been told that they think we do not care about manure as much as they did. . . ."

Master Gather, the resident guru on governing the castle, shifted his considerable bulk on a stool that did not look like it could last much longer, and said, "Yes, today's peasants (and even the younger vassals) are different. For one thing, they are not tolerant of the old culture, they just do not relate to it. Their whole life does not revolve around the castle; they have other interests, and want more time to spend with their families or whatever they spend time with. More of them are women and people from other lands. They do not accept and wish to ignore the old ways of doing things. They do very much care about the castle's health and future, but they have a much different perspective than our old lords."

Mistress McMethod remarked, "The sense of mission of the average lord seems to stop at the end of his desk. We all have that perception, whatever the truth may be."

"Right," Mistress Win cried, "I do not know how they can think ill of us when 'tis so obvious that they themselves got where they are by most shamelessly caring less about manure than about their own careers."

"Sometimes the same thing," muttered Ironbottom.

"Their real problem is not us," Master Gather said, "it is really that there are too many lords and too few towers." He grinned and they all smiled at the classic conundrum of bureaucrats. "The lords cannot or will not understand that the new generation is very different and so continue to insist on everything being done their way."

Mistress McMethod, a serious and intelligent student of castle dynamics, interjected, "They may not take their people very seriously, but at least the lords have instituted affirmative action programs for people who are different, and a program to help peasants and even vassals."

"Bulldroppings!" cried Ironbottom.

"The Technical Trap," Gather said intensely, "and an unseemly blend of misguided attention and facile lip service it is indeed."

"Bulldroppings!" cried Ironbottom again. "We do not need a Technical Trap, which is just a way to trick us into being satisfied not being a lord. No, what we really need is a miracle that would make lords better managers."

"We are now in competition," continued Thomas, ignoring the remarks, "competition with the rest of the empire and indeed the whole world beyond (whatever that turns out to be). Competition requires creativity, responsiveness to our customers, and the best use of our resources, especially our human resources. There is a chasm in perception, expectations and communication between the lords and us. We spend too much time and energy on internal warfare, both between horizontal units and vertical classes.

"While we are expected to hold down costs and sacrifice, the lords continue to live luxuriously, their own compensation increasing with no relationship to their effect on the castle's production. In fact, they do not give us an example by which to guide our own conduct. Certainly not a good one. They are profligate, spending pots of gold by whimsy.

"We need to work together, to learn from each other; synthesize the two cultures into a better castle. We need a revelation statement on what the tower (and the castle for that matter) should become. The lords must agree upon it. Then the statement must be sold, not with a perfunctory proclamation but by presenting it repeatedly at every opportunity. The lords must believe in it and communicate that belief to the rest of us. The revelation should be an active reference point, a bench mark against which to measure all that we do."

Thomas became silent, looking at the hands now quietly lying in his lap, allowing his words to sink into the youthful minds of the subdued vassals arrayed about him on their elderly stools.

"Well, it seems that the answer is near at hand," said Thomas, looking facetiously at the group around the long, thin table they had jammed into their cubicle (once everyone was seated no one could move, unless they all did), "the lords have discovered the panacea." Thomas paused to let the anticipation build, "And it is called *reformation*."

"Bulldroppings!" cried Master Ironbottom. His roar echoed around the table. "It should not surprise us that we have come to this point. The lords take to reformations like our King Arthur takes to every fad diet that comes along . . . and with the same result. They just will not admit that any organization needs strong leadership and good governing; that any organization will work well with those attributes, and any organization will fail without them."

Thomas stood up and looked earnestly from one to another of his compatriots. "I agree," he spat. "Reformation is not a *panacea*, moving offices and people around does not bring with it fundamental change. Our behavior does not grow from rules, laws and *structure*. No, the truth is exactly the opposite. We must change ourselves before the elemental nature of the castle can change. Previous reformations of the castle have been superficial. The lords shuffled the pieces around but did not fundamentally change the nature of the pieces.

The moral: One thing is clear, either we govern change or change will govern us and win.

The Parables of the Tail with No Teeth, Part VI

The Tale of the Rearranged Tooth and Tail - Reunions

The SAVEiors met with the Prince of the Piles and his Princepals almost every week. The meetings were very much like all meetings in the castle.

The SAVEiors met in the prince's private meeting room, which was called the Hall of Martyrs. The hall had been named for the many Princes of Piles that reigned one after another without visible effect on operations in the stables.

The Lords Princepals always vied with one another to be the last to arrive. Each did this to prove that he (there were no she-lords) was busier than any the other lord. Some meetings started very late as a result.

The SAVEiors controlled the nameplates that were placed before each lord to show his seat. They shuffled them constantly, trying to account for which lord was mad at which other lord at the time of the meeting. The only other item on the table was Mistress Win. The winsome Win sat smack upon the middle of the table, legs crossed, parchment, quill and a huge pot of ink ostentatiously arrayed in her lap. Mistress Win recorded every word spoken at these meetings, to avoid the confusion of poor or selective lordly memories.

Thomas always led each meeting with a summary of what the vassals had done for the lords since the last meeting. His tactic was to involve the lords by ascribing every SAVEior action as a charge from the prince or his lords. The prince always agreed with what the vassals recommended then did the opposite. The lords, some of whom were actively opposing the whole process, bobbed and weaved awesomely to avoid being associated with any decision Thomas presented. They were never overtly negative but, as the Lord of North Stable had once blurted out, their lack of disapproval was not to be construed as approval.

Lords had vice-lords that sometimes attended meetings for them. But on this day something extraordinary happened as all the lords and their vice-lords were expected. The prince was to be there (which at least partly accounted for the full attendance) and so were his aides. The Lord of the Rod arrived just before the prince. He led the prince's private retinue, his staff (of which SAVE was part), arrived first. He liked to think of the SAVEiors as his children and tried to be encouraging, which was often necessary.

The Lord of the Horde, Lord Bellicose, arrived shortly after. He was in charge of the Knights of the Shield who provided protection for the castle. He was also the prince's liaison with the kingdom's Knights-Errant, and his chief military advisor. (The Knights-Errant were a very large producer of manure and a potential rival for the castle.)

As each lord arrived there was a momentary shuffle as each tried to find the chair he had been assigned this time. Sir Rodney Longnose arrived first and his retinue quickly sat in the gallery. Sir Rodney was Lord of the West Stable. He was a soft, insecure man who made up for his lack of character by engaging in constant, manic and uncontrollable falsehoods. He lied about everything including the weather. He was so afraid of the truth that he could look you in the eye and swear it was snowing during the ides of July.

The Lord of the North Stable, Sir Leslie Slimelips, followed behind Sir Rodney closely. Sir Rodney was widely recognized by the vassals as the most incompetent of a largely incompetent lot of lords. Sir Leslie compounded the effect of his ineptitude by being incapable of delegating control of anything. Just to add dash to this pitiful potpourri, he was a thief who stole every perk the castle had to offer and more.

A few minutes later Sir Linus Limpwrist, Lord of the South Stable, sauntered in with his usual large gaggle of aides. Sir Linus was a sly, devious man marvelously adept at avoiding decisions. This helped him create an unbeatable record of avoiding blame for the disasters that inevitably occurred in organizations during his reigns, or just after he left them. He avoided controversy like the plague, which always seemed to follow just behind him. His retinue took places in a corner, far from the others in the gallery.

Finally, just before the prince, the Lord of the East Stable swaggered in leading the largest of the personal gangs present on this day. The group was large both in number and in size. Some of the men looked to be thugs from the worst streets in the village, mean, evil, and suitably intimidating. Sir Howard Fleetsmile was a bully and liked to have plenty of bullies around him. He was a hard, inflexible man, who hated constraints and never accepted advice from anyone other than superiors. Sir Howard was the most dangerous man in the room because he could be wrong, do wrong and not care a whit. He was merciless.

These men, with their faceless and largely voiceless vice-lords sitting beside them, chattered and joked to pass the time while they waited for the prince to arrive. The oft-comatose Vice-Lord of the West Stable, the only lord officially recognized as senile, promptly fell asleep and except for an occasional bout of snoring, was not heard from again. The vice-lord had once slept through a SAVE recommendation to kill his favorite program. He then assailed Mistress McMethod, complaining that no one spoke up in favor of it. The good Mistress tactfully refrained from pointing out that it might have been a nice idea if the vice-lord himself had done so.

The prince always tried to be the last to arrive, although the Lord of the East Stable sometimes beat him at this game. On this day the prince won and rushed in breathlessly as though having hurried from another very important meeting. (Actually, he'd forgotten about this meeting and had to be awakened from his midmorning nap.) As he often did he immediately apologized for his tardiness, and then declared that he had an important disclosure to make. Mistress Win pointedly poised to capture the words.

"Despite all rumors to the contrary, I am *not* planning to retire," he announced, eyeing the lords for any signs of disappointment in their faces. But he was the disappointed one this time. He'd pulled this trick once too often; after many such experiences the lords had caught on and now only stared back impassively.

"Bulldroppings," muttered Master Cutpurse under his breath. He was the SAVEior from the Tower of Gold whose Lord of the Hoard loudly disrespected the too profligate Prince of the Piles.

The prince bleakly motioned for the proceedings to proceed. Thomas always started the meetings with introductions of any new vassals masochistic enough to join the SAVEiors. On this day he had one to make. "Today we are happy to welcome Master Gibbet, representing the Lord of the Horde."

Lord Bellicose beamed. "Raison d'etre," he said proudly to no one in particular. He had sent Gibbet to make sure that SAVE did not cause the Knights-Errant to attack the castle.

"And now the commercial for this week," said Thomas, gesturing to Mistress Lorelei to hold up a large placard upon which was inscribed in bold letters HE WHO DOES NOT PLAN FOR THE FUTURE, HAS NONE. (Lordly attendance at the SAVEior meetings had increased markedly after Thomas had begun to use the comely Mistress Lorelei as his placard holder. The lords looked at the words, then at each other in embarrassment. Most did not know how to plan, which of course is why the SAVEiors existed. Those lords who engaged in any activity remotely resembling planning did so only to further their own careers.

Thomas hurried on. "We also met with the Suicide Group and gave them our recommendations on the closing of castle annexes they are studying for you."

"Who," the prince looked puzzled.

"The Suicide Group? Operation Hangman? You set them up to help you decide which annexes to close and which to keep or change."

The prince turned to the Lord of the Rod and still looking blank, whispered, "Look into this strange assemblage, will you. It does not sound familiar to me." The prince's memory was well known to be as long as his attention span, neither of which was very lengthy.

Mistress Lorelei held up another placard as Thomas continued. "And, in our usual review, here are the results of last week's meeting. These are the agreements that you all made." Lorelei lowered the placard and her décolletage simultaneously. "And," she raised the same placard again, "here is the list of those which you subsequently changed your minds on."

The Lord of the North Stable shot back, "As I have said

many times before, nothing I say or do not say can be construed to be acceptance of any agreement made at this table. I do not even agree with the seating arrangement this week." The lord folded his arms and sat back in his chair smugly, with the SAVEiors staring at him in utter amazement.

"Bulldroppings," Master Cutpurse made his usual succinct commentary.

SAVE was now working on identifying the issues inherent in a comprehensive reformation of the castle, and the resulting upheaval to its workers. It was becoming quite clear to the SAVEiors that neither the prince, nor his lords, had any intention of making any real changes in a system that had benefited them so well personally. They also had no interest in making big changes to a hierarchy in which they were so well situated.

"Our first presentation for you will be given by Master Gather, who has been studying the effects of reformations on other castles. He is in charge of our touchy-feely studies and will tell you of traps we must avoid if we are to succeed."

Master Gather heaved his bulk to its feet. Beard trembling in his earnestness, he began. "Reformations cause people pain. No matter how necessary they are, or how much the people want them, there is an inevitable apprehension. Sometimes they become so upset that they cannot work as well. They need to be helped, cared for, and considered." As he continued the eyes of some lords glazed over, others began to look increasingly impatient. Finally, the prince pounded his fist on the table.

"You mean to tell me that my vassals are a bunch of softies? Why, when I was young vassals were tough, they could take anything!"

"And had to," Mistress McMethod whispered to Thomas behind her hand.

"I do not want a bunch of wimps in my stable," interrupted the Lord of the East Stable.

"Raison d'etre!" exclaimed Lord Bellicose.

"Indeed," the Lord of the North Stable shouted.

"If they cannot stand the smell, they ought to get out of the stable!" exclaimed the Lord of the Reap.

"Bulldroppings," roared the Lord of the Hoard.

"Raison d'etre," Lord Bellicose agreed.

"This is why the peasants are trying to create a 'union,' the Guild of the Lily," McMethod whispered, loudly this time, at Thomas.

Stunned, Master Gather's voice trailed off, ". . . and we should set up a special effort to help them. . . ."

Lord Bellicose hooted, "I will help them all right!" He turned to the prince, "give these whiners to me, my lord, I can always use more cannon fodder."

Amid the furiously nodding heads about the table, Thomas leapt up to change the subject. Master Gather sat down with a sigh; he was deciding to shave off his beard so that the lords couldn't recognize him at the next meeting.

"Next we will hear from Mistress McMethod, who will tell us about the opportunities that the reformation will hold for our Technical Trap program," Thomas urgently gestured for McMethod to begin quickly.

Casting a baleful glance at Thomas, McMethod reluctantly got to her feet to address the angry lords. "The reformation is our opportunity to revitalize the Technical Trap—"

"What is wrong with it," the Lord of the South Stable broke in, "I designed it and I think it is doing an admirable job of keeping the vassals in their place--er, I mean, giving them good places!"

"With respect, sir, the Technical Trap is an admission of failure, failure of the castle to sustain an atmosphere in which those who handle dung could grow and be rewarded. The lords and their tower sycophants have status and gold; the vassals in the stables have only more dung."

"*Only* dung," cried the prince, "only dung? By all that is holy, what is wrong with that? Dung is what we are all about. Without dung, where would we be? I love dung and so should they. I love the smell of it in the morning. They should consider themselves lucky, I would give up my crown to trade places with them--to exchange my soulless piles of gold for a good warm, steaming pile of dung." Seeing the lords looking at him in shock, he hurriedly, if lamely, added, "Of course, that just is not possible. My destiny is to lead, to sacrifice my dung heap for a throne."

"Um, yes, of course, sir, and we all admire you for your sense of sacrifice. It is well known in the stables." Thomas looked desperately about for the next speaker.

"Bulldroppings!" Master Cutpurse was becoming louder out of frustration.

Master Ironbottom jumped up and hurried to the head of the table. He was a very brave vassal. "We must show a clear change of direction! No business as usual, I say! Clearly, the East Stable must give up everything." He looked challengingly at the bemused lords and abruptly sat down.

"Raison d'etre," muttered Lord Bellicose.

"Indeed," cried the Lord of the North Stable.

"I believe I just heard your brain fart, young man," declared the Lord of the East Stable.

"Sounds like a good idea to me," muttered the Vice-Lord of the North Stable, who was sitting next to the Lord of the East Stable.

The Lord of the East Stable whirled upon the vice-lord, reached for his sword, and shouted, "We will see who gives up what! Your manure is just like ours. I will make sure you lose just as much as we do!"

Master Ironbottom again jumped to his feet and, holding up a large placard, yelled at the top of his lungs, "Here are the vision, goals and strategies we recommend for the reformation, my lords. Please give me your attention."

The Lord of the East Stable, suddenly embarrassed, sat down

heavily. The Vice-Lord of the North Stable, wincing, clambered out from under the table and regained his chair. The other lords, trying to regain their self-control, pretended to pay rapt attention to Ironbottom.

Pacing back and forth in front of the table, Master Ironbottom intoned, "Yes, my lords, the reformation requires flexible efficiency; adaptive dynamism; proactive consolidation; reduction, combination and augmentation of everything; shifting improvements of all developments; and, most of all, reconstruction and preservation to ensure the—"

"Excuse me, young man," interrupted the Lord of the North Stable, "what the devil are you talking about?"

"He *is* giving us the general situation," explained the Lord of the South Stable.

"Well, I want specifics."

"The last time they gave us specifics you turned them all down," remarked the prince, looking at the lords disgustedly.

"That is why I want him to get specific, so I can know what I am turning down," asserted the Lord of the North Stable.

The Lord of the West Stable spoke for the first time, "I might only be a little lord of a little stable but I think what we need is a fused report putting all the elements of activity together. The whole picture, you know."

"Of course, what a wonderful idea," harmonized the Lord of the Rod, who played Whist with the Lord of the West Stable, "I will get right on it." He looked at Thomas conveying the clear message that "I will" meant, "*You* will."

"Furthermore," said the Lord of the West Stable, who was an intellectual, "we must decide what our manure requirements are to make sure that we are shoveling the right, er, uh, stuff."

"We already have, sir," said the prince, "I approved the list just the other day."

"Yes, my liege, but it was not the list we made for you, you know, the one you approved two months ago," interjected Thomas.

"But you agreed to my list a month ago," cried the Lord of the East Stable.

"What happened to *my* list?" asked the Lord of the North Stable.

"Um, yes, of course, gentlemen. You all have different lists. But no matter, I decided not to rank this latest list. I took off all the numbers. Now it is just an alphabetical list." The prince looked about triumphantly. This, indeed, was a decision worthy of Solomon, he thought.

"You what. . . ."

"SAVE had no trouble ranking them. We voted," interjected Master Ironbottom.

The Lord of the North Stable suddenly looked apoplectic. His face red, eyes bulging and temples throbbing, he shouted, "You voted? Voted! Great creeping radicals." Turning to the prince, finger waving accusingly in the general direction of the SAVEiors, he intoned, "You see! These folks are v-o-t-i-n-g? No wonder they make decisions. Well, I for one will not stand for it. They cannot make decisions for me. I have the right not to make my own decisions. *I* am an *adult*. These vassals obviously need *adult* supervision." He sat back exhausted.

"Well, I do not know if it is all that bad," the prince said distractedly. "At least they did what I asked them to do. I did not tell them that we had to like it."

"We must have priorities and they must accord with the Unified Game Plan of the King," insisted the Lord of the Rod.

"We cannot reform according to that plan," replied the prince.

"Why not?"

"Because we do not have one."

"Oh."

"Did you lose it?" asked the irrepressible Master Ironbottom.

"No, the King and his court could not agree on one. Now they're working a *Confederated* Game Plan," replied the unfazed prince.

"Well, one thing is clear, they sure have many sacred cows," stated the Lord of the Rod.

The prince turned on him and, his voice rising righteously, insisted, "We have no sacred cows. I will not have it. Everything is on the table during the reformation."

"Even Project Rip-Off (E)," queried the Lord of the East

Stable.

"That is an exception"

"Operations Shipwreck, Mistrial?"

"Exceptions."

"Well then, how about Minormode or Carry-on-throw-Off . . . or the Superabacus Palace," joined the Lord of the South Stable.

"I did not mean them," the prince said firmly.

"Surely we can get rid of Quicksand/Semester or Robin Pint or that crazy Gadfly project," insisted the Lord of the West Stable.

"No, of course, not."

"Then certainly Fisherman and Blarneybag can go?" asked the Lord of the North Stable desperately.

"Um, actually, no. The King really likes them . . . but everything else is fair game," the prince sat back with finality.

"There is nothing else," remarked Master Cutpurse, the SAVEiors' pots of gold expert.

The prince decided it was time to change the subject. "What we really need to do is move parts of the stables around. Shake things up. Get, what is that word, efficiency. We need efficiency. What about Smoke and Mirrors?"

"Huh?" A dumbfounded Lord of the Rod couldn't help himself.

"Smoke and Mirrors, I said. The two wise men. I understand they came back after the king beheaded Fog and Smog, the wise men that had replaced Smoke and Mirrors. They always have the answer.

Whenever we do not agree on something, they are able to make it look like at least something happened. They call it perception management. Repackage the same contents--maybe even less content--packaging is important, they say."

"Yes, my lord, you mean yell *before* we feel pain . . . like we did during the Gold Ration process," remarked Master Cutpurse.

"Um, something like that," replied the prince, shifting uneasily in his throne-like chair. "We did what we had to. We made up a Gold Ration for the King that looked different but really was not . . . to protect the castle and the stables."

"Yes, my lord, but by reducing everything the stables needed, the good and the bad, instead of eliminating the least useful, you hurt us all," said Hal of Heedless. Heedless was not happy with the progress of the reformation.

"Maybe, but I hurt you all equally, and do not forget it," rejoined the rapidly angering prince. Thomas jumped in to forestall a likely confrontation and, waving another chart in the air, he cried, "Gentlemen, our time is short. We must return to the subject of this gathering, the reformation. Lord Magnet, Holder of the Horses for the Lord of the East Stable, has graciously consented to address us on the results of his Kitten Team efforts to find the causes of the bloat and excessive layers of bureaucracy we have in the castle."

"Kitten Team?" Howard Fleetsmile, Lord of the East Stable, sometimes seemed to be the only lord paying attention.

"I'm sorry," Thomas gulped, "I meant Cat Team . . . Crisis

Action Team." He had been caught using one of the disdainful SAVEior terms for ineffectual bureaucratic nostrums employed by the prince.

The prince, looking less than pleased—was it with Thomas or Magnet—interjected that he was very sorry but he had to leave soon and perhaps the good Sir Magnet could hurry through his presentation leaving out unimportant elements, such as any conclusions he might have.

Lord Magnet, slightly disconcerted but determined nonetheless, quickly agreed and launched into a monologue to the obviously uninterested lords around the table. He was a member of the oxymoronically named "Junior-Seniors"--newly anointed members of the aristocracy--who formed a group known colloquially as the FATSO (Functionally and Technically Too Staff Oriented). The King, at a recent Kingdom Conclave, had a sudden inspiration for another study. Looking around the meeting hall for anyone who might still be capable of a little work, he espied a small handful of youthful looking nobles sitting in the backbenches. They never had a chance.

"Gentlemen, I have read all there is to read on the subject," declared Magnet, holding up a thin sheaf of parchment sheets. "It is obvious that we have too many horse holders," the lords began to smile, ". . . and too many nobles," the smiles disappeared, "in the castle," Lord Magnet finished.

"In the castle," asked the cagey Lord of the North Stable,

"but not in the stables?"

"No, of course not. We in the stables do all the principal work for the castle. No. On the contrary, we need *more* lords here." Lord Magnet grinned in triumph as the lords joked and laughed among themselves about how to convert more horse holder appointments to the nobility.

"Gentlemen," the prince raised his right hand. "I hate to break into your dreams but let me point out that the King runs the castle, not we here in the stables. The support towers outnumber us, in towers and advisors on the King's Council. We do not have a ghost of a chance of selling this idea anywhere else in the castle."

"Well then, let us take over . . . with a coup de manure, as it were. We will tell the King to go fly a goatskin. What can he do? We have all the manure in the castle under our control. We have *defecational* hegemony!" The Lord of the North Stable was not well known for his tactful insight into castle politics.

"Forget it!" the prince said firmly. He was used to these feculent interruptions. "Do you have anything else to tell us, Lord Magnet," the prince spoke as he was gathering up the parchment notes he'd made during this the latest encounter with the SAVEiors, who he was beginning to suspect of latent disrespect.

Lord Magnet began speaking very fast, while furiously sailing one placard after another at Lorelei as he finished with it, in a largely vain attempt to get through to the lords.

"I was only japing you, my lords, actually we do not need

more lords, we need to increase the span of control of fewer lords," said Magnet to a puzzled looking audience.

"What is a 'span of control'?" asked the Lord of the West Stable, who had recently won 10,000 pieces of gold for being named Overseer of the Year in the castle. This reward went to the lord elected by his peers as the best manager in the past twelve months. In fact, they rotated the largess among themselves alphabetically.

"Raison d'etre," remarked Lord Bellicose knowingly.

"That is when you have more vassals working for fewer lords," answered Lord Magnet.

The lords of the stables looked completely flabbergasted, "But how can we run every last detail of the manure production that way?" they asked in unison.

"That is the point, my lords," responded Magnet, "you do not, and you should not You should be giving the vassals more responsibility--and the authority to go along with it."

The lords looked at each other in utter consternation. What was this man talking about? We cannot trust the vassals, they are nowhere close to as smart as we are; they need *adult supervision*. Magnet must be one of those wild-eyed liberals from that effete university in the east. Obviously the King made a mistake raising him to the nobility.

"Well, I must be off," said the prince, standing, "I must inspect the north fields. The peasants there need my help and advice badly. Is there anything else, Master Thomas?"

"My lord, we have presented many important points, many of which we did not have a chance to discuss but are in the parchmentwork we are passing out to you all now. We need decisions on them and tasks assigned to carry them out."

"Write them up in an Inaction Memorandum, Thomas, and I will sign it next Wednesday," the prince threw the words over his shoulder has he hurried from the room.

McMethod turned to Thomas, "But I thought the prince was leaving for Italy Tuesday."

Thomas looked at the ceiling and shrugged his suffering.

The moral: A decision avoided is a decision made anyway.

The Parables of the Tail with No Teeth, Part VII

The Tale of the Rearranged Tooth and Tail - Counter-Reformation

As planning for the castle reformation continued it became clear that the average lord's view of new ways of doing business was to take someone else's manure production and add it to his own empire. The predicament was an age old one: who was to be in control of what. Everyone agreed that *something* had to be done, and leaped upon every opportunity for another study, but no one could agree to any specific proposals to *do* anything.

The axe was falling and few wanted to be under it.

Sir Lancelot knew where it was falling and visited the SAVEiors in their dungeon in the Catacombs. As always it was cold and damp--water constantly dripped from the ill-fitted stones--and stank of the oil lamps the SAVEiors used to fight back the gloom. Lancelot brushed aside an incipient mushroom, sat down and came right to the point.

"We have lost," he said wearily, "we have failed to change the direction of the reformation enough for it to really change anything. The lords, who didn't want the reformation anyway, have not been able to agree and cooperate among themselves on an alternative. So it has come to pass that, despite the unresolved issues, a reformation will come to pass." The SAVEiors smiled tentatively.

"Unfortunately, it's turned into a counter-reformation," Thomas said.

The SAVEiors groaned.

"Furthermore," continued Lancelot, brushing dust from his velvet jacket, "the prince has decreed that the reformation will occur along functional lines. Thus, all care and feeding of the manure producers will be consolidated in a single stable. All collections and processing of the manure will be placed under one lord in another stable. Another stable will do all packaging and delivery of manure. He also plans a fourth stable, the stated purpose of which is to process manure supplied by the Knights-Errant. (The sole purpose of this stable seems really to be so all of our esteemed lords can retain their present towers.)

"Then, because the prince's new brother-in-law, Sir Guile the Guilty, needs a sinecure, he created a fifth stable. The prince told me, 'I'll figure out what to do with it later.'" The prince thought he had agreement for this from the lords of the stables, but the lords fought the creation of another stable when they discovered they would lose parts of their own stables to make it. Nevertheless, after many heated battles, the lords have finally worked out a series of compromises (which benefit only the current lords) that allow the reformation to continue." The SAVEiors groaned again.

Lancelot flicked a cockroach from his britches with a look of utter distaste. "Predictably, the manure graders who, as you know, engage in a very specialized class of work requiring a very unusual class of vassals, insisted that they needed their own tower. The prince acquiesced and will build them the Tower of Manureology. The manureologists have immediately and naturally set about building their own empire. They insist they know better than anyone does how to grade manure and will not allow the stables to interfere. It is obvious to me that eventually they will become totally independent . . . and uncontrollable."

"I am afraid you are right, sir," said Thomas, crushing the offending cockroach beneath his slipper, "and we are beginning to see other manifestations—as opposed to the infestations we suffer in this putative work space of ours—we see already that the lords are taking advantage of the movement of people to rid themselves of deadwood."

"That is the term they use for everyone who does not agree with them," interjected Mistress Win.

"Most really were not dead, of course," explained Mistress McMethod, "just unhappy, mismatched to job and disaffected."

"The lords are complaining about receiving cast offs even as they are vigorously engaged in casting off their own undesirables," finished Thomas.

"We are calling this period of the reformation—counter-reformation—the FADE, the castle's Free Agent Draft Enactment," wisecracked Master Tarnish.

"Yes, and the many fights occurring over vassals and their billets will engender ill will that I am afraid will become a permanent fixture in the new stables," declared Sir Lancelot. "As you all know, the prince has insisted upon a strong body of minilords and vassals to reside in the Tower of Feculence and protect him from the lords of the stables. They are still called the Special Taskers of All Foolish Fiefdom Silliness, but will have even more power than the unseemly power they had before."

"Right," said Thomas, "and to protect themselves from staffs, and to carry on the infighting with the other stables, the lords of each stable are building their own large staffs. They are called hidden staffs because the reformation is supposed to avoid the necessity for them and they were forbidden by the prince."

"The problem is," said Master Extort, "no parchmentwork, no matter how insignificant, will leave the Tower of Feculence without every lord and every lord's hidden staff having touched it first. Soon there will be so many different points of coordination all of which can say no, only one or two of which can say yes, that nothing very important will ever happen."

"So what is new?" asked the cynical Master Tarnish.

"Hidden staffs will exist only to give every lord power over every other lord's actions," concluded Master Extort.

"Success had a thousand lords, failure only one lord scapegoat," sighed Thomas. "Well, let me thank you all for what you've tried to do," Sir Lancelot said after a pause. "The lords are smart enough not to balk the prince head-on, so they sent talented, if expendable, people. I don't think they knew how good you were."

Sir Lancelot coughed. "The air is very bad in here. You need some fresh air." He sighed, "I am angered that the King can allow the Lord of the Flush to claim he has solved the pollution problem." He coughed again, more strenuously. "I must leave this space," he said as he rose to leave. He paused at the door, looking at each SAVEior meaningfully in the eye, and said, "And I think you should, too."

The lords based the reformation on premises dealing only with things. They did not affect at all the culture of inefficiency. Much of that inefficiency stemmed from the lack of decision making in the whole castle. Decisions were made late, inconsistently or not at all. The vassals were forced into much extra work, most of which was wasted, providing alternative and contingency plans while awaiting outcomes that they could not predict. Nowhere was the wasted time more evident than in the Gold Rationing of the Munificence Cycle. Fully half the work done was directly due to the lack of clearly stated goals and strategies. The reformation changed none of this. On the contrary, it exacerbated the problem in the stables, because the entire process had been fractionated, and the overarching need for corporateness could not be achieved within the castle's culture of every man for himself.

The very lexicon of the castle evolved during the period of the FADE and its aftermath. "Flexibility" became the code word for avoiding decisions. It was used instead of "management." Lords "obfuscated" instead of "decided." "Responsibility" became "blur," to describe the diffusion of responsibility that was rife, especially in Gold Ration actions. "Actions" was never used; it was replaced by "delegation," by which the lords meant only responsibility, not authority. The words *duty*, *service* and *mission* disappeared altogether. The lords just said, "I want."

A major reason for the castle's past inefficiency was its high lord-to-vassal ratio. As downsized vassals left the castle but the number of lords remained the same (they weren't forced to leave), the ratio continued to worsen. Lords fought duels with each other for the few remaining lucrative sinecures.

The supporting towers of the castle--towers such as Plumbing and Stalling--had long been taxing the stables for everything they did for them. They not only got their own pots of the castle's gold from the gold ration process, but could charge an extra fee to the Tower of Feculence for anything anyone there asked for. They could then spend their extra gold on their own desires. Every support tower did the same, which made already gold-starved stables poorer: the teeth starved while the tail grew long and opulent.

Many vassals lost their place in the castle hierarchy and had to accept lesser positions. The reformation plan called for many vassals from the East Stable to move to other stables, since it assumed that there would be less need for its manure in the future. Many vassals from all the stables and towers controlled by the prince had to move to the new stable serving the Knights-Lanced. They named it the Horse Stable, since the knights were only interested in horse manure. The Knights-Errant—the manure collecting arm of the Knights-Lanced—took all the good jobs in the Horse Stable and ambitious vassals soon learned not to work there.

Every stable insisted on collecting its own fodder. Despite a primary reason for the reformation being efficiency by centralizing fodder collection in the Horse Stable, no lord trusted the Knights-Errant to supply the right fodder at the right time. Many fights broke out in the fields around the castle when foraging parties from the stables ran into each other trying to reap the same grain. Because the prince could not impose central control, the internecine fighting continued ever more bitterly.

The struggle over which stable could spread what manure reached epic proportions. The denizens of the South Stable claimed that they alone must spread all manure that resulted from processing fodder from their fields. The East Stable, which used everyone else's fields as it wished because the king had always favored it over the other stables, insisted that all fodder suited for its type of manure was its to process and spread alone, no matter whence the fodder came. The manure was fractionalized beyond its integrity and often worked over so often by so many stables that it became sterile.

The idea of organizational standards had not attracted much attention during reformation planning. Moreover, the functional approach allowed each stable to claim to be unique. So they grew independently and acted independently. Everyone had authority over the walkways that linked the stables but no one had responsibility for them. The grass grew high and the underbrush encroached. Negotiating these connections became very difficult and few tried. Before the reformation each stable controlled its output from tail to teeth. Now they always had another stable to blame for failure. Personal and organizational accountability atrophied. Finger pointing became the favorite exercise of the stables.

It so happened that during this time the latest management fad in the neighboring castle was something called the Mattress Organization. It promised efficiency, although little else, through centralization of effort and sharing vassals. The aptness of the name became apparent as soon as the lords tried it. It became clear very soon that it allowed the lords to feather their own beds. Every lord depended on the other lords in the Mattress to operate all stables but the first priority of every lord was his own stable. Trust, cooperation and planning were essential to the success of the Mattress Organization. The Prince was forced to abandon the idea forthwith.

The Prince has hoped to adopt techniques during the reformation to enhance the lot and productivity of vassals throughout his dominion. This too was subverted by the lords, who managed to continue to handle vassals as they always had. They did this through a grand sounding program known as Personal Enhancement Techniques nicknamed PETs because only vassals who pleased the lords were able to take advantage of it.

The lords also rid themselves of the SAVE, something many

of them had been trying to do from its very beginning. They convinced the prince that they had jobs for the SAVEiors even more important than planning. They made the remaining SAVE vassals, Stewards of the Stalls. The prince had promised them all responsible service when they left SAVE. The lords were happy to keep this promise for him; all the former SAVEiors were responsible for keeping the stables clean. Only Thomas à Bucket was spared this ignominy. Sir Lancelot kept his word and brought Thomas back to the Tower of Power as his personal valet. (His elevation turned out to be geographic only.) Sir Lancelot had decided to lie low for a while, awaiting another opportunity for revolution. In the castle it seemed planning for the future had no future.

The final blow landed when suddenly the farmers needed the manure from the East Stable again. The prince found that he had gotten out in front of the peasants and the Knights and they weren't following. They needed more not less East Stable manure and complained to the King when they couldn't get it. The King, who had originally agreed to the cutback, demanded to know how the Prince of the Piles could be so stupid to run out of East Stable manure.

So it came to pass that the Tower of Feculence acquired a metaphorical stench not unlike that of its main product.

In desperation the prince called upon the wise men, Smoke and Mirrors, for the answer. "What can I do," he said glumly, "my princedom is in shambles and is threatening to cease functioning altogether? It is obviously time for another solution."

Smoke and Mirrors thought for a moment, and then replied brightly, "It is obviously time for another reformation."

The moral: We must manage change or change will manage us.

Any organization, whatever its makeup, needs to inculcate a sense of participation in its workers. Primary ingredients of a healthy organization: trust, mutual support, and the sense of total mission are not automatically included in the benefits of reorganization. Unless the organization changes the culture also, dysfunction will follow. Reorganization cannot be a substitute for strong leadership and good management.

The Parables of the Tail with No Teeth, Part VIII

A Tale of Teeth Decay Prevention

Once upon a time, a castle stood in the midst of fertile fields in the Land of Red Tape. It was a very big castle with a huge complex of stables. The stables produced large amounts of manure, rare manure. Castle manure was uncommon in the kingdom because the king did not allow anyone else to own the kind of animals raised there. The food these animals ate, even the process by which the food was transformed into manure, was kept secret. The Tower of Power vetted all the people who worked in the stables of this castle. No one else was allowed into the barns. Spies were everywhere; one could not be too vigilant.

Inevitably, because of the ensuing inbreeding of animals, not to mention lords, the quality of the manure began to wane. As customers began to complain, the prince and then the king became alarmed. After trying but failing to gain any progress through his Knights of the Conference Table, the king finally consulted his Wise Men, Smoke and Mirrors.

Smoke immediately saw the solution. He went to his Trunk

of Trigraphs and pulled out the first few sets of letters that caught his fancy. He showed them to Mirrors.

"Hmmm, let us see. WOE, Wipe Out Ennui? No, too French. PVH, Push Vassals Harder? No, too hard to do. Ah, here is one: TQM! Tower Quality Manure?"

"Yes, that is it," cried Smoke, "Tower Quality Manure. Nothing like a catchy abbreviation to give the illusion of progress until this ill wind changes direction."

The Wise Men giggled as they hurried off to see the king.

Months after the Great Reformation, the placement of vassals and peasants still had not been nailed down. This afflicted period became known as the Billet Ballet, because every tower in the castle was supposed to have a fixed number of cubicles, which were called billets, and the lords danced them around repeatedly as they sought to gain *billetal* advantage.

During the Reformation, which affected the Tower of Feculence most, new stables were built and the stalls were changed around in the old stables. All this meant that the allocation of billets to each stable differed. The old stables were reluctant to give up their billets to the new stables and resorted to all sorts of subterfuges to hide, thus keep them. The new stables had trouble finding billets for all the animals and vassals they were supposed to house.

Soon vassals and peasants were moving about and working in stables without regard to how many billets there were. Many swore allegiance to one stable but worked in another because there were no billets in the right stable. Large stables lost billets and had plenty of room left over; smaller stables gained inhabitants but not billets or stall space and were crowded. The prince and his lords exerted no effort to fix this sorry state of affairs, since they knew they could never achieve a consensus on what to do. Besides, they all had billets and very nice ones at that. Although self-restraints were anathema to the lords, they had no difficulty applying very severe rules of behavior on others. Rules had become the lifeblood of castle commerce. The entire castle staff subsisted on rules, or so it seemed to the king and his Knights of the Conference Table. The years of improving production had coincided with dizzying growth in the number of regulation promulgated by the king. (The same era was known as the "Age of Excess" because a munificent emperor had kept the castle well supplied with pots of gold. The Knights of the Conference Table ignored this because they could make rules but not gold.)

Faced with imperative change, the lords naturally chose to meet this latest challenge the only way that they knew how, with more rules. Thus it came to pass that castle culture and TQM clashed in titanic struggle for the rights to castle management: who would lead, who would follow and who would have to get out of the way.

The peasants and many vassals joined the TQM camp at first. They wanted to believe the smell of change in the air would not dissipate into the stench of disappointment, so they enthusiastically pitched in to make TQM work. The lords, who wanted only to see pitch forks in the hands of peasants, not suggestions, were dismayed by what they had loosed. They didn't have to worry long. The inept, almost contemptuous, implementation of TQM soon killed all enthusiasm and progress . . . except in the Tower of Plumbing and Stalling.

Quality in Tower of Plumbing and Stalling products was easy to measure. The pipes and the cisterns either leaked or they did not. Poor quality induced an immediate reaction from damp customers, brandishing sodden mops, gave voice to their disappointment in the tower's handiwork. In contrast, the stables of the Tower of Feculence could produce manure of widely varying quality, the blame for which results could be easily blamed on poor application or bad weather. The Lord of the Flush had nowhere to hide and therefore embraced TQM, and was the only lord to do so for very long. The king put the Lord of the Flush in for the Emperor's Quality Improvement and Productivity Award. The castle didn't excel at much but it was well known for its excellent plumbing.

As lords other than the Lord of the Flush, began to suffer organizational agonies, the king resorted to the beefed up Parchment Patrol to solve the problems. Parchment Patrollers consisted of the lowest level of the peasantry, who worked in the shadows of every corner of every tower of the castle. They were lackeys who could achieve self-respect in no other way than to insist on their bureaucratic prerogatives. They enforced the Dictat Bureaucratica. The king, prince, and lords, wasted no respect on these misanthropic minions, but regularly used them to do lordly dirty work. The Parchment Patrol took over the TQM process.

A torrent of TQM flowed from the top to the bottom like wine through the press, until it hit bottom and splashed any unwitting peasant and vassal in the way. The pace was so fast that none of the juice lingered above, not even a stain. Few nobles were tainted by the idea. The lords breathed a collective sigh of relief when it was clear the king would actively push TQM no longer, missing the unintended effect of the emptying of the TQM pitcher: the nobles could hold the vassals responsible for TQM while continuing business as usual themselves.

Our hero, Thomas à Bucket, withstood the onslaught of TQM for as long as his 'bureaucratics' threshold could, and then repaired once more to the chambers of his friend and mentor, Sir Lancelot.

"Hello, my son," cried Lancelot as Thomas crossed his threshold, through the door and into his attention. "Come in, come in. To what (let me guess) do I owe the honor of your company, lad? It would not be the latest trick of Smoke and Mirrors, would it," winked Lancelot.

"Right as usual, sir," Thomas sighed as he picked his way through the shells of illicit walnuts on the floor. Sniffing the air and pointing to the dirty straw on the floor, Thomas asked, "What in Merlin's Name has been going on here?"

Lancelot smiled ruefully and explained, "For a while there the Billet Ballet caused me to have to share my chamber with a horse. We got that straightened out in a hurry, I can tell you."

Thomas shrugged, "The Billet Ballet was another problem TQM could not fix."

"Ah, but you misunderstand, my boy. TQM does not *fix* anything. People must do that. TQM is common sense, but more than that it is a process that seeks to improve process, a structure upon which to hang common sense principles. It is a mechanism to accomplish what one hopes to do, plans to do, trying hard to do the best he or she can."

"Sort of people pulling together, toward common purposes, helping each other. No wonder it does not work here." Thomas winced to think what people could accomplish in the castle if they were not so worried about getting the credit themselves so that they could be better off than anyone else.

"There are exceptions. Exceptional people. Even lords, me lad," Lancelot mused. "Remember how all the lords in all the towers helped vassal Harold the Halt through those rough times when his wife was so sick? The inclination is there; we just have to find how to turn the exception into the rule. Most lords are not bad people, just bad lords."

Thomas nodded dubious agreement as Lancelot shook himself out of the reverie. He slid the walnut bowl across his desk to Thomas. "Now we have another glitch in the saga of TQM in the castle," he grimaced. "While the king and Prince of the Piles both pepper their speeches (when they think about it) with references to

TQM, it turns out they do not mean the same thing when they say it."

His fingers wrapped around a large "TQM" walnut, Thomas looked a question at Lancelot.

"When the king speaks TQM he uses all the words the wise men invented. This seems to be because he does not understand a word of it all, but repeats what his two closest aids tell him. I mean His Eminence Grise, Cardinal Wooly, and the Royal Factotum, Sir Guy of Good, the godfather of TQM in the castle. Unfortunately, the king grew up in another castle. He doesn't mean the same thing the words he is given mean. Confusion, not the king, continues to reign over us."

Thomas, mouth full of walnut meat, could only vigorously nod his knowledge of these two famous and influential figures in the Tower of Power.

Lancelot added another degree of grimace to his face and said, "These gentlemen, Sir Guy in particular, are enthralled by the ideas of the Wise Men and translate their every utterance immediately back to the king. They may have the best in their hearts for the inhabitants of the castle; but they cannot control the nobles between them and the peasants. And the lords are not so willing to share their power and perquisites with *rabble*."

"The Prince of the Piles, on the other exquisitely manicured hand, understands perfectly well when Smoke and Mirrors prattle on about acceptable manure quality levels, customer requirements and expectations, error detection or prevention (usually applied as prevention of error detection), and the like," explained Lancelot. "He is just convinced that he has a better idea."

"Yes sir, we have noticed in the stables," exclaimed Thomas in recognition of another human foible, "The prince was groomed from birth to be a prince. He has taken his turn as lord of many of our towers but has never actually had to shovel manure or deal directly with peasants in anything other than a master-slave condition."

"Yes, I have had many a conversation with him, Thomas," said Lancelot beckoning for the walnut bowl, "He believes producing manure is easy, requiring little more than the application of an abacus to make things come out well. He regards making manure as a science needing only enough gold, instead of being the art it is; therefore, needing talented vassals."

Sir Lancelot fished out an especially large walnut and smashed it on his table with his gold nutcracker with the castle's flag emblazoned in silver upon it. "He, like many lords, is simply viscerally unable to admit any other ideas into his mind without first stamping 'my idea' on them. Very much a lordly trait. Thus, the dreams of TQM—especially empowerment of the commoners—are anathema."

Lancelot rose from his special issue Lord's Minithrone, complete with permanently attached flagpole. Fiddling with the folds of the dun colored castle flag, he continued, "Once our prince commissioned a group of vassals (the king forced him to it) to investigate a problem and report recommendations back to him.

According to the tenets of TQM, they were called a PIT, expanded by the lords into a Primarily Inactive Team. They were supposed to be empowered to fix the problem, but according to the tenets of the lords, all vassals by definition require 'adult supervision' from a lord. So all they could do was recommend, nothing more. Lords can be empowered sometimes, never vassals.

"None of their suggestions comported with what the prince thought was proper. Despite TQM's dictum to accept one of their offerings, he summarily refused all, summarily had the group executed and, in summary, never tried that again."

Sir Lancelot looked up, as Thomas made ready to leave. "You have picked an excellent time to travel away from the castle, Thomas. Mayhap all will be well when you return." Lancelot smiled, "Well, maybe just a little better."

It had come to pass that our hero, Thomas à Bucket, was to travel to other castles to bring word of his new conveyor belt-aided manure handler to the castle's envoys. He had known that his first hurdle was the finite amount of gold available, and that lords liked to travel. Of course, trips by lords had first priority; vassals could use only the gold that was left over. Thus, lordly trips always took precedence and necessary trips by vassals often could not be made. Thomas had resolved not to bother Lancelot with this problem but, at the mention of it, couldn't resist. "What advice can you give me to get through the parchmentwork needed for authorization of my trip," he said quickly.

"Well, Thomas, my good lad, they will probably turn you down automatically. Will not even consider how necessary the trip is. You see we are now in that period at the end of the Castle Year when the importance of a trip is directly proportional to the rank of the traveler. The higher the rank, the more likely the approval will be given."

"In other words, the real importance of the trip is *inversely* proportional to the rank of the traveler," remarked Thomas.

Ignoring this impertinence, Lancelot shifted in his chair, sending a shower of walnut shells flying to the already littered floor. "So it seems. And to make matters even worse, the Power Tower is being penalized again for having managed its travel funds in a responsible way," he said. "We controlled our travel gold carefully, spread the trips out over the whole year, and saved some back for any important trips that might come up at the end of the year . . . like yours.

"Others, who spend profligately, without thought or planning, are now in need of more gold. They will be given some of ours so that the prince can keep everyone happy. That never works, but we will be punished anyway, in essence for having followed the king's guidance to spend carefully. Those who ignored him, and continued to spend as fast as possible on anything they felt like, will be rewarded by receiving our remaining gold."

"Is it true that if we do not use up all travel gold the Lord of the Hoard allots us for the year, then the Lord thinks we do not need as much the next year and shortchanges us during the next Munificence Cycle?" asked Thomas.

"Yes, it is true. And not only that, but if we plan to use so much gold for a given trip, and tell the Golden Tower, then do not use that much—perhaps because we found a way to save gold (usually at cost to our own comfort)—we do not get to keep the gold we save. We have to give it back to the Golden Tower, which then saves it for other lords to use.

"Someday we will give up and join the problem instead of fighting it. Then we will spend just as fast and wastefully as the others do. Then the nobles will not be able to understand why their orders to save are not followed." Lancelot slapped his fist on the table, wincing as shards from the walnut shells there bit into his flesh.

"This state of affairs is ripe for an approach by TQM," said Thomas, trying to ignore Lancelot's obvious discomfort and embarrassment. "A quality approach would dictate that incentives to save be instituted. Perhaps by promising that all gold saved by a tower will go right back to that tower to meet its own future travel needs."

"It will never happen," gasped Lancelot through pain frozen jaws.

"Why on earth not?"

"Because the money now saved is placed in a slush fund pot for the exclusive use of lords."

"But if I go to a rentahorse counter and accept a nag at less gold than the Golden Tower allocated, the stable ought to get that money back for another trip," insisted Thomas.

"I did that once . . . when I was young. The Lord of Boondoggles' minions in the Tower of Tours erred and did not make the promised reservation for my two traveling companions or me. Only a tiny, broken down old nag was available--all three of us rode on it to save money. It was the last time I did that because soon after I found out that another lord had upgraded his horse to a stallion using the gold we saved."

Thomas, against all odds, did make his trip and when he returned, he immediately repaired to Sir Lancelot's chambers to learn what had transpired with TQM during his absence in the hinterlands.

Lancelot was talking with Sir Louis Fitz Tails, the king's Keeper of the Coin. Fitz Tails was a very busy man for, under the rubric of Tower Quality Manure, he facilitated decision-making conclaves of the lords. He always carried The Coin with him in a velvet purselet hanging around his neck like a badge denoting his decisive importance to the castle.

Fitz Tails was talking about his most recent bout with lordly judgment making as Lancelot motioned Thomas to enter. "So the prince and the lords of the stables argued over the three-stage improvement of the stalls in the West Stables. They proudly announced agreement (The Coin came up heads) on the first stage, which was easy for it called only for planning, not spending gold.

The problem is that was all they could agree upon. Even The Coin could not overcome their reluctance to commit themselves to helping one stable over any other."

Fitz Tails wryly scratched his curly, black hair as he concluded his story. "Finally they accepted that they were only agreed that there would be two more stages but would not agree on what they would be."

"That is a fine example of the paralysis consensus decision making can cause," Lancelot said as he shook Thomas' hand. "But you may not have heard the latest, Fitz. The Prince of the Piles, shortly after his ruling to do it, followed up with the new decision not to do it. Coincidentally enough, he did so right after giving the Lord of the South Stable a singular audience.

"Yes, 'The last lord heard, is the successful lord'," muttered Fitz Tails as he left the chamber.

"And the last shall be first," Thomas muttered.

"Sit down, me lad," cried Sir Lancelot as he simultaneously waved goodbye to Fitz Tails and welcome to Thomas à Bucket. "We have no time to chat today. I have an important job for you, one which you must begin immediately."

"Yes, sir," nodded Thomas.

"This is what you must do. I am giving you my warrant to take TQM to the lords of the towers. I call it a 'Quality Council' and you will be the facilitator. Matters are going from bad to worse in the castle—not just in the stables—and we have to do something swiftly."

So it was that Thomas found himself at the head of the very large meeting table of the king. Minilords representing each tower occupied the many chairs around him. They were not the lords that Lancelot had hoped for. As soon as the lords found out the subject of the conclave, and that the king would not be there, they all sent their profound regrets that attendance, their personal attendance, would be impossible. But, of course, they said they would send their closest associates—lieges well versed in the thoughts and intentions of the lords themselves.

Thomas explained to the minilords why Lancelot had called the Quality Council. He listed a number of the problems that cried out for attention, TQM or otherwise, anything but inaction was appropriate.

He talked of the eight elements of managing Tower Quality. When he offered the idea that leadership to achieve quality improvements must replace lordship, their reply was, "Are you implying that the lords are not providing the best possible leadership now? How can we tell them they have erred? No, not us!"

When he explained how they needed to organize for quality improvement, they said in unison, pointing at each other, "But that would mean my lord would lose autonomy, would be forced to consider others and be more disciplined in approach. The other towers may need to do that, but not us."

When he said that tower quality education was at the heart of the drive for quality, they said, "But who will be working while so many vassals are in school? And another thing, you cannot expect lords to go to school. The castle would fall apart. Anyway, lords already know everything important there is to know. Maybe a few peasants can go, but not us!"

And when he spoke of customer expectations, conformance, communication with and between the towers, they scoffed, "Our customers do not know anything. The only conformance we need is for everyone to do as the lords say. We will communicate their orders and that will be that. Change the way we are doing things? Not us!"

Finally, he appealed to them to take action and to begin by developing a plan. They readily agreed to plan, for they knew that planning was a perfect excuse for inaction. There is not enough information; we need to look at another angle; the right people have not seen this, we need to include them (thereby starting a new round of meetings). Such are the cries of the progress busters.

Thomas had already concluded that the lords had prepared too well the minilords they had sent to the Quality Council. None were empowered to make any contribution except "No!" The lords continued to substitute *emasculate* for *empower*. Nonetheless, he persevered.

The stable employed many vassals and peasants to package and distribute the manure. Some had to live in other castles because the manure was so unique that its use required special techniques.

124

These individuals--known as the Fielded Authorized Remote Manurists, or FARMers, because they were experts in the producing and using of manure--had to work with the peasants of other castles to make sure that the manure was used correctly in the best possible way.

Vassals were posted to other lands for a few years by means of Horizontal Extra Realm Transfers (pronounced by the vassals as hurt, which is what happened to them when they returned to headquarters). Re-assimilation caused vassals to lose their places in tower pecking orders while away from the bureaucratic fray. The FARMers were often completely forgotten by lords who had no use for what these vassals might be doing—helping others to use the castle's products, for instance. They also didn't care about the experience the vassals accumulated while doing it. Lords preferred to deal with only one culture at a time.

Tainted by foreign dung or coming back believing such hideous abstractions as *the customer is always right*, the returnees were nothing but trouble in the eyes of the lords. The first thing they did to each one was to have them re-dipped in the castle's manure. Most then walked the stony halls of the castle, begging friends, acquaintances and just about anyone who would smile at them, for a billet.

"This seems to be a prime subject for a Tower Quality Improvement Project for the vassals," said Master Thomas. "Our objective would be to reclaim one hundred percent of the returnees into useful employment within the castle, and to plan so that we do so as soon as they cross the moat."

"That has already been tried," interrupted Sir Hal the Heedless, from the Tower of Collections. "It was the Universe Program and it degenerated into a rubber-stamp of whatever decision on people placement the lords wanted to make. We called it The Lottery because the odds against a vassal winning a good position through the program were astronomically against him. It competed with lordly prerogatives and failed. What can we do now that would be any better?"

"The Project will tell us that," ducked Thomas.

"Ha! Bunk, my dear vassal," exclaimed Lady Barbara of Banal, from the Ivory Tower, "and who will listen to mere vassals when they are done?"

"You will," Thomas answered, grinning in triumph, "you all will as members of the Tower Quality Steering Team that will lead the effort."

Sir Gilles of Gumshoe, sent by Lord Peek, standing and making ready to leave, expressed the reaction of all. "If you think any of us is going to risk a promising career by telling the lords what to do, you can guess again. You vassals need more, not less, adult supervision," he flung over his shoulder as he joined the throng leaving the room.

"Not I!" resounded separately and in unison into the hallway.

Lady Barbara was famous for having mothered the Ivory

Tower course on *Communications Skills*. This ill-thought out, and just as ill timed, course advertised instruction in how to give and receive criticism and to improve communications with lords. The course did not last long for lords liked to give criticism to vassals, but found receiving it back to be completely unacceptable.

Thomas sat paralyzed in the king's chair. His eyes were aimed at the doorway but were not focused there. *What a fine disorder Sir Lancelot got me into this time. We do not have any quality to manage in this castle. TQM is doomed.*

Thomas' pessimistic and cynical appraisal proved to be accurate. The more pessimistic and cynical, the more accurate it seemed. As soon as the lords saw what a threat Tower Quality Management was becoming to their privileges, they quickly set out to consign it to the 'offal pile' of history. The old king conveniently died and the new one, wisely under the circumstances, wasn't as keen on TQM.

The lords were greatly helped as TQM was gradually discredited through inappropriate and incompetent application. The vassals chosen to facilitate its inculcation often were chosen by their availability, not qualifications. Even when competent, dedicated vassals were mistakenly chosen, they soon lost heart in frustration. The general lack of discipline—top down and personal—also insured failure. TQM assumed restraint already existed, and did not encompass the theory to create it.

The Ivory Tower, having earned a well-deserved reputation

of transferring ignorance rather than knowledge, continued to demonstrate how far it had been left out in the fields when it solicited students for a course called *How to Play the Game*. It purported to help vassals develop personal plans to pursue career goals in the face of royal policies and procedures. The king with no prodding from the lords killed this one.

Filling classes that the Ivory Tower wanted to teach, but to which the other lords did not want to send vassals, was one of the problems the Wise Men solved for the Lord of the Ivory Tower. Their solution was awesome in its simplicity, and mind boggling in its cynicism. They simply declared all unpopular courses to be prerequisites for the other, more popular, courses. The other lords, busy with what they considered more important matters, didn't notice. Such courses were easy to teach because so many educationalists, vassals too old to work in the stables any longer, were available to teach them. The classes were offered many times a year.

When the Wise Men invented the Indenture Program, designed to ensure the proper preparation of promising vassals for Transubstantiation (ennobling as lords); they inadvertently struck pay dirt for the Ivory Tower. Vassals began to take every class they could, whether or not it had any relationship to their job. They justified the need to attend them by claiming a right to be allowed to qualify for Transubstantiation. The Lord of the Ivory Tower, Sir Simple Simon, saw the advantage of not looking the gift horse in the mouth and increased the numbers of classes, and his staff, quickly. One regrettable result was that because the indentured had priority, few others could attend the classes they needed for their current or next level job. Another burr in the vassal saddle.

Thus, Tower Quality Manure inadvertently became the catalyst for increasingly vocal expressions of dissatisfaction from the lower ranks of the castle. The king and the nobles had envisioned bottom-up energy to carry out top-down commands; they had not counted on the depth of unhappiness TQM unleashed. The lords feared insurrection and wanted the TQM process stopped immediately.

A small group of lords, terminally fed up, hired the formerly discredited wise men, Fog and Smog, and asked them for a way out of conundrum. The wise men thought for a while, grunted, and gave birth to a new acronym, CIM (Castle Information Management). The lords loved the sound of it; managing information (they knew that knowledge was power) was what they were very good at.

Thus it came to pass, that the new king was moved to declare that Tower Quality Manure had been a complete success. He thanked everyone for their unstinting efforts to make it so. He announced that he was propelling the castle onto the next plane of operations through the "twice distilled quintessence" of TQM, CIM.

The lords were thrilled; the vassals yawned.

The moral: He who would lead a bandwagon must first make sure all his horses are going in the same direction.

TQM required attributes the lords of the castle would not supply: sympathetic understanding, enthusiastic acceptance and disciplined application. But, of course, if these attributes had existed in the first place, the castle would not have needed TQM in the first place.

The king liked TQM because he thought he could wind it up like a clock, pay lip service to it (fit it into his schedule every Thursday afternoon), but not have to change fundamentally what he did, or how he did it. TQM seemed an outside force exerting pressure on management (lords) and vassals (middle management) alike, without any close and abiding leadership attention from him. But TQM, like so many of these palliatives, is really only one view of common sense dressed in a new and fancy costume.

The vassals grew to dislike and deride TQM because the poor implementation did not impart the improvements they were promised. To them it was soon clear that the behavior of vassals and peasants was the target of the modification, not the lords, who in fact were not changed by it at all. Thus, albeit for different reasons, no one in the castle was happy with TQM.

Finally, bureaucracies are sustained by rules--the Dictat Bureaucratica of the castle. Rules are the vitamins of bureaucracies: the more rules they ingest, the larger they grow. Bureaucracies seek to improve effectiveness by applying new rules; the more they try to improve, the more rules they pile on. Unfortunately, just as too many vitamins are inimical to humans, so too many rules cause bureaucratic paralysis and failure.

TQM aspires to the release of the whole individual to achieve a greater common good. Bureaucracies seek to be more proficient by fettering the individual in rules and regulations, also for the greater good. This does not create a propitious environment for TQM.

As always, the potential for progress lies in people. The definition of progress lies in leadership. The successful bonding of the two elements occurs through shared values and goals.

The Parables of the Tail with No Teeth, Part IX

The End of the Tail Tale

Once upon a time, a castle stood in the midst of fertile fields in the Land of Red Tape. The aged castle was nestled on a high promontory deep within the well-paved bosom of the Land of Red Tape. Once it was a fat castle, rich and powerful, but now it lay in ruined splendor. It had been stripped of many of its building stones and all of its dignity. Grass grew where grass had not been allowed to grow during the castle's hay days. Vines smothered the work of generations of castle planners.

Three strangers stumbled over the pebbled remains of once mighty towers as they picked their way to the castle's gate. "Look," cried one, as he pointed at thin entrails of smoke rising from the seedy gatehouse, "perhaps someone still lives here."

As the astonished strangers stumbled up the remaining path to the castle, an old man wearing a patchwork quilt for a robe peered from the dark gap marking the entrance to the rotting gatehouse. Quickly recovering from his surprise, the elder stepped forward into the sun. The ancient apparition's lowly vestments could not mask his noble bearing. His white hair surrounded his head and face so lustrously it must be clean. The vermin that were surely the only other inhabitants of the castle's crumbling shell did not inhabit him.

"Well, hello to you, my most honored huffing and puffing visitors," the old man gracefully opened his arms in welcome. "You must be well tired and thirsty from climbing the ruined hill to my likewise ruined abode. Do come in and share a spot of most assuredly unspoiled mead with me."

The strangers followed the old man into his bare but immaculate apartment. They looked at each other and the same questions appeared in their eyes. As this evident keeper of the castle turned to motion his visitors to be seated upon the benches along the walls, he spoke in a strong and clear voice, "I will answer the questions in your eyes. Clearly, I do not see many that understand language, mine at least, and I look forward to conversation with you. My name is Thomas, Thomas à Bucket, and I am the only living bureaucrat remaining on this hilltop. I do not count the squirrels; although I must admit that their bureaucracy is much more effective than ours was."

Whilst handing cups of sweet mead to each of his mesmerized guests, he spoke again, "And to answer your second question: I own this castle. I once served it and now I command it . . . what is left of it anyway. But to answer your third question would take longer, longer than a cup of mead takes to drain." He sat down at the small desk in one corner of the room, under the light of a large window. He reached into a large wooden bowl and picked out a small, oblong object.

Thomas' guests said almost in unison, "Please tell us anyway, dear Thomas à Bucket."

"We have come a long way from the university to study these ruins, Mister Bucket, and we have all the time you need," said the man who appeared to be the leader of the strangers.

"Call me Thomas," smiled Thomas à Bucket, keeper of the castle. "I believe you must be learned men and therefore willing to learn the lesson in the sad story of this castle's last throes and final death. I will tell you that story gladly, but first you must promise me to retell it at every nonce and chance. As you can see, once fallen, a castle does not again arise. I can only hope my story helps prevent the decline of yours from starting at all."

The strangers look at each other wonderingly.

Thomas picked up a mallet and crashed it down on the thing he had plucked from the bowl. His guests could now see that it was a walnut, which had long been illegal in the kingdom. Their curiosity being stronger than their legal concerns, they held their lips and paid full attention to the beard out of which came the following melancholy tale.

"This was once a thriving castle," began Thomas said, "that produced manure that flowed freely and abundantly across the moat and to our customers far and wide. All the inhabitants of the castle, lord or peasant, worked hard and together to make the stables the best in the kingdom. This arrangement worked very well in the early years. Too well, I think. The stables were so successful that the Emperor was convinced to make a good thing better by making it bigger. I now know that this was the beginning of the end for the castle. Press gangs ranged about the empire bringing into servitude all manner of human being, whether suitable for the castle or not. The emperor, trying to keep his subjects happy, decreed that all should work. But it did not matter at what, and the castle eventually became a vessel of misfits.

"The lords were nonplussed since, they had been hands-on-manure experts who received little or no training in commanding man or horse . . . and who had only bad examples to follow. The new men they had recruited to join them in the Tower of Power understood something of overseeing peasants, but absolutely nothing of manure. They were also nonplussed. Over the years, all and sundry had withdrawn farther *and further* from the manure piles, which stench they ceased to abide. The fundamental purpose of the castle was now lost from sight and mind.

"The King of the Castle, a Knight of the Conference Table, tried to rejuvenate production the only way he knew how: He tried to impose a systematic approach upon the day-to-day workings of production, which was an art, not a science. Engineers loved this solution because it seemed to create bureaucratic perpetual motion. Lords loved it because perpetual motion promised results without undue involvement.

"The king's wise men had invented Transubstantiation, by which promising vassals would be identified and prepared to manage the stables . . . and personnel management could be put into perpetual motion also. The lords dispensed Transubstantiation as alms to anyone loyal and uncritical, and further watered down the lordly substance.

"Meanwhile, the castle itself was growing exponentially in size and complexity. So too was the production of manure. With so much energy misdirected away from the waning quality of our output, which became watery as a lord, the dilution was finally noticeable even to our least observant or caring patronage.

"With Transubstantiation seemingly a success (lords were attracting sycophants like flies to a horse's rear); the king asked the wise men to concoct another perpetual motion, this time to identify men for knighthood. These so-called wise men created the Senior Nobles' Order of Bosses—we irreverent vassals shortened that to SNOB—by which every lord could be better than the other. This move created a caste system that hastened the demise of the castle."

The strangers stirred uncomprehendingly.

"Oh," Thomas quickly said, "this was because now the lords concentrated most of their energies on something much more important than manure, their careers. SNOBery replaced good manure as the preeminent reason to work in the castle. Most decisions were made with respect to the relevance to the Order of Bosses, not the orders of customers."

The strangers nodded and relaxed again in their chairs.

"The king," Thomas resumed his woeful tale, "with his ill-advised attempts to improve things, was in fact choking the life blood from the castle by wrapping miles of red tape around its throat. Not unlike so many other reformers before and since (who also failed, I can't help noting), he denied the existence of human nature and acted as though platitudes could save the castle.

"Of course, the newly minted lords also had to have important positions. Soon for every SNOB the king created, he also had to create a new billet—at the bottom of the ever-expanding hierarchy. And of course every new position added to the bottom, especially the functionary appointments, raised the importance and altitude of the offices above it (many of which quickly became sinecures).

"Some of the new functions and offices thus created were so useless that they were nicknamed benefices (bennies, for short) by increasingly cynical vassals." Thomas grimaced at the memory.

"The castle's environs also grew dramatically as all the newly created bennies required new towers to be built for them. When new towers could not be built fast enough, some were created out of stable spaces, further constricting production of manure. The king had his princes rent space in the castles of other kings, which took more gold out of this castle and fattened the coffers of ruthless men gleefully taking advantage of our king's mismanagement.

"Within the castle, unfortunately, red tape continued to grow almost exponentially. Fostered by the egos and insecurity of the lords, it soon was found in every nook and cranny. The red tape slithered across the floors, up the walls and across the desks of every vassal and peasant. It wrapped itself around wrists and legs of servants, and their piles of parchmentwork. It crept into the compartments of nobles and wound around the necks of lords, shutting off the flow of thought-giving blood to their heads. When the king tried to beat back the advances, the red tape encircled his arm and prevented him from unsheathing his sword. It was sclerosis of the castle-livers and a bureaucratic collapse of epic proportions.

"I could go on but I think you can clearly see the downward spiral the results of which you now see before you. It took many years but it was inevitable."

Thomas raised his hands, shrugged his shoulders and let his hands fall into his lap. Then he motioned to the mead jar, the question in his eyes.

The strangers held out their cups and the leader urged, "Please do go on. We come from a kingdom far away in miles but very close in manner to what you describe."

"All right. It is painful but if it will help, then I will." Thomas plucked another forbidden enjoyment from his bowl and resumed his reminiscence.

"Successive kings tried all the myths, all the quick fixes to improve production. The wise men came up with a never-ending stream of palliatives that promised at least the appearance of change but did not overtax valuable lordly time with such trivial pursuits. T-Groups and Lordly Grids, Matrix Lordism and Zero-based Munificence Cycles, Quality Circles and Tower Quality Manure . . . each one came and each one left again, usually without leaving a trace of its passing. (Who can see lost opportunity?) Meanwhile, one philosophy—most definitely not a myth—prevailed. Careerism (do you have such a word in your lands?) flourished without any help at all from the wise men. It burgeoned because of all the cultures possible, it is the one that grows best when no attention is paid to it.

"Many princes realized the worthiness of that most pleasant of irrelevancies, study. These lords created study group after study group. There were so many study groups active over so long a period that they began to study each other's studies. Each group was unique in composition and approach but they all shared two things in common: they took much longer than planned to make recommendations (I guess they did not want the fun to end), and their recommendations were always ignored. Study groups have only one purpose: to delay action. The lords loved studies.

"The last king seemed to know something had to be done but he had already choked on red tape too long. His judgment had been impaired by his insular career as well. He no longer could think clearly; only his own career achieved sufficient clarity in his mind to be dealt with competently.

"But he did finally assign progress (although of what was always equivocal) monitoring duties to his Tower of Power. However (in my most humble conviction), he fatally stabbed himself in the foot with his longsword when he, on the advice of his Knights of the Conference Table, bade the Power Tower to stay away from anything to do with gold or the peasantry."

"Why?" interrupted the leader of strangers.

"What was the Power Tower?" asked another.

Thomas rose to refill outstretched cups. "I beg your pardon, gentlemen. I forget you have no knowledge of this castle then or now. The Power Tower and Tower of Power are one and the same. It was the grandest tower of all because all the grandest lords maintained their headquarters there. The king's apartments were on the top floor. We vassals usually called it simply TOP, which was always said with a note of disdain in the voice."

Thomas sat again as the strangers nodded and indicated he should continue. "Why? Because the lords had convinced the king that these were too sensitive for unnoble monitors to know about. All those still capable of rational, independent thought were not allowed to cross the moat."

"Ah, so the rulers continued to hide from their responsibility—and anyone who might remind them of it—and deny their accountability. Yes, this is typical," the leader said, his words almost lost in his copious beard.

"My champion," Thomas was nodding his head, "Sir Lancelot, was put in charge of the monitoring because all the other lords considered it a waste of time and thus perfect for this most vexatious (to them) of all nobles. As usual, he called me in to help him."

Thomas' gaze left the room and fixed upon a point beyond his window. "I remember him greeting me as he always did, 'Well now, my good Thomas, it is most pleasant to see you. Sit; sit down here next to me. What can I do for you, young man?' he said as he sat heavily (his aging bones always ached now) on the divan next to me. By this time he was losing his memory, if not his mind, under the pressure of almost single-handedly trying to keep the castle together in the face of such massive inertia.

"I softly reminded him that he had sent for me, which launched him into his statements (without the slightest sign of embarrassment, I might add).

"'Thomas, we have our work cut out for us this time.' That meant that *I* had *my* work cut out for *me*. 'The king has knighted me as Lord of the Ombud. I must listen for complaints and report them to him.'

"'What about fixing problems?' I said innocently, knowing what the answer must be.

"'He did not mention fixing anything, young Thomas, just

reporting the situation to him,' said my mentor. Then he looked up and realized I could not have been serious, having been around for a while. Then he said, and I think he was smiling, 'Maybe I am really Lord of the Snitch, eh? Oh, well. Nonetheless, the lords will try to keep me, us, from seeing any problems, of course. And the king himself has tried to tie our hands even before we start. He giveth with one hand and taketh with the other, eh? Ah, yes. Well, the misuse of gold is rampant through ignorant and misguided spending, but I do not believe we face a criminal situation there. The misuse of people, though also not criminal, is very much immoral—and will destroy the castle someday if we do not check it now.

"'The lords wish in particular to hide the billet ballet that they have been dancing for years. Contrary to kingdom policy, no relationship is allowed between the billets that limit how many workers a prince can have, and how many bodies he can stuff into a tower. This allows the lords to *appear* to be managing well—by cutting billets for instance—while not really cutting back on the actual number of peasants working for them in the stables or towers.

"'It is so bad that the emperor is cracking down and even the king and Knights of the Conference Table now have to get out of their privy and do something. Some of their towers were supposed to have been torn down, but they continue to operate anyway with people who have no billets at all.'"

"The lords," Thomas contemplated, "also played a game of Musical Towers. They constantly reorganized the towers seeking the magic combination that would cook well without key ingredients such as good management. They never found one. As Sir Lancelot had said many times, 'No matter how much they moved the animal cages around, the castle was still a zoo.'

"The castle's dispensaries were always full of vassals suffering anxiety problems (including heart attacks) and our General Surgeon's tents were swamped with vassals and peasants who could no longer cope with the strain.

"'We have to do something, sir,' I told Sir Lancelot, 'because being a vassal like me means being in the middle. The lords above me lie and try to hide facts from me and the peasants below me also lie and try to hide themselves from me. I usually feel like I have been run over by a horse and carriage . . . in both directions.'"

"'A clear case of shit and run, I am sure,' smiled Sir Lancelot. I knew his crude use of language and attempt to make light of my plight meant he was also bending under the pressure."

"I remember Sir Lancelot breaking open a walnut with his yellowing teeth (he was very well practiced in the art). He looked up at me and wanted to know what the peasants thought about the Lord of the Abacus' latest costs-cutting ploy. (Of course, that particular lord always shared in the savings, particularly when he prevented raids on the king's treasury by minions bent on wasting it in the stables. Sometimes the reward was more gold than the idea saved.) Anyway, this was a sort of self-help program where instead of providing expertise and strong arms, the lord merely gave the peasants permission to do the work themselves . . . and sometimes also pay for it themselves.

"I still remember Sir Lancelot's wicked smile when he asked, 'How do they like being given so much unprecedented *freedom*?'"

Thomas grimaced at the bittersweet memory. "I could not help replying," he said, "that they saw it for what it really was. They had their own name for it, the 'You Are on Your Own Now!' policy."

"Well, Thomas said after a long silence the strangers were careful not to disturb, "the 'do-it-yourself-if-you-want-it-done' policy meant that the Tower of Feculence, under which the stables now labored, lost all support from the castle. What little support remained was needed to take care of the Tower of Power, of course. 'TOP would stay there until the end,' Sir Lancelot said more than once. Meanwhile, everyone in the Tower of Feculence lost subsistence in direct relation to his perceived castle importance.

"Emergency support went first. Whenever something broke that affected production, the vassals sent a runner to the Tower of the R&D—Rework and Diddle—to request help. The lord of the R&D Tower, Lord Fiddle, had won the power struggle over who would get to wield what little remained of support in the castle. All too often, scribes of Lord Fiddle would tell the runner, 'Sorry, We are too busy to get to it now. We will call you when *we* are ready.' So, it came to pass that production statistics in the stables came to be driven by the Tower of R&D, not the Prince of the Piles and his stables. The priorities of the castle came to be driven by its Tail, not its Teeth.

"On the other hand, the Tower of R&D loved to find modish 'things' to build for the rest of the castle. Often before anyone in the stables knew they needed anything new or different, peasants from the Tower of R&D would appear with equipment in hand. They would demand to be allowed to replace older tools with the unaccustomed invention of some parchment-pusher in the Tower of R&D. Just as often, the new apparatus did not work as well as the old without the loss of much blood and sweat . . . and time. Thus, production in the stable suffered more during the interminable 'break-in periods' thrust upon it by Lord Fiddle and his minions from Hell.

"Then Lord Fiddle, suddenly aware of self-help's threat to his newly acquired importance, issued a Princely Ban on all self-help within the castle. This effectively brought a halt to any work in the castle that he had not authorized. The Tail was very important indeed. In such ways each tower created its own agenda and these programs of the Tail competed all too successfully with those of the Teeth of the castle."

Thomas à Bucket rose and shuffled to the wash table. He splashed a ladle of water into his face and returned to his chair. He sat again, water droplets slowly escaping his beard.

"I reasoned," he continued, "and Sir Lancelot agreed, that a solution to the problem could be found in creating a King's Edict forbidding Lord Fiddle and all the other Tails from possessing any gold of their own. If they had no gold of their own to spend, they would have to satisfy their human tendency to spend with the gold of others. Presumably then, the owners of the gold, the teeth of the castle in this case, would dictate what the Lord Fiddles could spend it on."

Thomas shrugged again. "But, as we should have known, the Tails controlled the king by now, and the idea never had a chance. Thus, the topsy-turvy world of the castle continued its downward spiral.

"Then," Thomas straightened in his chair and looked directly at the strangers, "in an effort to keep the Knights-Lanced—the king's own soldiers—from leaving the castle for good, many perquisites were given them by virtue of their "unique" training. Paladins were given more power than were ordinary vassals of the same rank. Paladins could command vassals but not vice versa. Unfortunately, Paladins came and went very fast. Their training was in demand and they sold themselves to the highest bidder . . . over and over again. They did not stay at the castle long enough to get to know their way around well. Their fealty was directed only to their own kind and so they never became a part of the castle culture. That is, until they took over and made the castle's culture the same as theirs."

Thomas spit this last statement out with quite evident contempt and disgust.

"Then the last king, who was also a Paladin, decreed that the castle's stables be torn down and the stones transported to the far ends of the kingdom to build new stables at the castles of other Paladin Kings. They were called such as Castle-West and Castle-East. It was the 'suffixiation' of the castle.

"The Emperor decreed that all the kingdoms must reduce the number of subjects employed within castle parapets. The empire suffered from gold drainage to other empires that could provide food and tools more cheaply than we could. It also suffered mightily from the drag of all those expensive suffixes.

"When finally forced to cut people, really trim, the king targeted the vassal class for extinction. Peasants could be counted upon to do what they were told, while vassals often thought they knew better than the NOBLEs. That was a pain in their priorities.

"The Wise Men, both Smoke and Mirrors, gave birth to another abortion: the Exfoliation Program. The king offered retirement gold and a cartload of manure to all that left the castle before their contract was up. (Vassals, of course, were oft the only ones who could afford to do this, since they were frequently close to the ends of their contracts anyway.)

"The collapse of the castle was thus accelerated.

"Many did not trust the king (who could blame them) and hung on to their billets with the obstinacy only bureaucrats can muster. Smoke then suggested the Double-Dipper program. [Thomas bestowed a rare smile on the strangers.] No, it is not a process in manure production. This was also known as the Feather-Bed Ploy and was a wild success since vassals, *and* NOBLEs this time, could terminate their contracts, get retirement gold AND continue working as before (only now their stipends were coming indirectly from the castle through the suffixes). Very neat and very lucrative, thus the highest vassals and dead-ended NOBLEs leaped at the chance to double the time they spent with their muzzles in the trough.

"Eventually the castle became only a small niche-producer of very specialized manure that nobody else wanted to bother with. The king was demoted to prince.

"Even that miniscule production was finally ended when entrepreneurs from the village, using the newest inventions, drove the castle out of that market as well. The prince closed the doors to the castle and joined the famous Diaspora Bureaucrati."

The strangers were nodding energetically in recognition of the denouement.

"All but my friend, Sir Lancelot. He was old and he was reminiscent and he bought the castle for just a few coppers."

Thomas looked up to see the questions arising on the faces

of the strangers. He stood up. "Well, you see, he died a few years ago and bequeathed this to me. This is how I honor his memory."

The moral: He who "vassalates," loses his castle.

Thomas' unfortunate castle died of Bureaucratitus, hardening of the hallways. This dread disease is carried by paper and can only be stopped by commonsense. That's why it is seldom defeated. But don't give up, dear reader; do not allow tails to wag the teeth. The antigen to Bureaucratitus is in this book. Find it, use it, and win.

Key to Parables' Names and Terms

Abacus, Lord of the - ruler of the castle's accounting department

Ad Hoc, Ibn - Prince of Production's chief advisor and golf partner

Arno the Lame - in charge of South Stable quick deliveries

Arthur of Arthritis upon Knee - the king of the castle

Arthur the Lesser - the king's son, Crown Prince and Prince of the Piles

Barbarians, The - inhabitants of the Middle Muddle

Bellicose, Lord (Horde)

Boondoggles, Lord of (Tower of Travel)

Bureaucraticus of Bloat - the castle philosopher of organization

Bureaucratic Police Force - the minions that labor in the shadows to ensure all goes according to the bureaucratic rules "Dictat Bureaucratica"

CIM - Castle Information Management

Clyde of Clod - supervising vassal in South Stable

Collections, Tower of (Lord of the Reap)

Conference Table, Knights of the (the senior lords)

Crystal Ball, Lord of (Tower of Tidings)

Debentures, Lord of (Tower of Debt)

Debt, Tower of (Lord of Debentures)

Dictat Bureaucratica - rules for castle operations

Dreams (budget submissions)

Dreams, Fiscal (the budget package)

Ductwork, Lord of the (Tower of Plumbing and Stalling)

Eminence Grise, His - Cardinal Wooly) (Informal deputy and close aid to king)

Factotum, Royal - Sir Guy of Good (Chief of Staff and close aid to king)

FADE (Free Agent Draft Enactment)

FATSO (Functionally and Technically Too Staff Oriented - the Junior-Seniors)

Feculence, Tower of (the four Stables)- led by the Prince of the Piles

Fiddle, Lord = leads the Tower of Rework and Diddle

Flush, Lord of (Tower of Tile)

Fudget (vassal nickname for the budget - see Gold Ration)

Gold Ration (Budget process)

Gold, Tower of - Treasury (AKA Golden Tower) (Lord of the Hoard) ((Formerly Lord of the Purse))

Grand Hall of the Treasure (Tower of Gold meeting room)

Golden Hoard (the treasure)

Goldkeepers - functionaries in the Tower of Gold

Hall of Martyrs (Prince of Power's Conference Room)

Hall of Flame = (the Flamers) in which castle's heroes are enshrined

Hearsay, Tower of = (IT-Information Technology)

Hoard, Lord of (Pot Tower)

Horde, Lord of (Lord Bellicose - lord in charge of castle's protection force, Knights of the Shield, and military advisor to the Prince of the Piles

Ibn Ad Hoc = Prince of Production's Moorish advisor and golf partner

Indenture Program (Intern Program)

Ivory, Tower of (Institute of Very Organized Readying of Yeoman)

Ivory Tower, Lord of the

Joint Chiefs of the Knights = leaders of military forces

JUMBLE (Joint Uniformed Manure Baggers Liaison Element) - the military's field liaison organization

Keeper of the Coin - Castle's decision-making facilitator (Louis Fitz Tails)

Knights-Errant - manure gatherers for the Knights-Lanced

Knights-Lanced - kingdom's military

Knights of the Shield (castle's protection force)

Land of Red Tape (in which the castle lies)

Manureologists (from Tower of Manureology)

Manureology, Tower of (for new Stable)

Mattress Organization = matrix management

Michael Angelo (does the briefing materials for the castle)

The Middle Muddle (the land of the Barbarians)

Munificence Cycle (budget cycle)

Ombud, Lord of the - Sir Lancelot's final position as ombudsman for the castle

Paladins - computer geeks

Parchment Patrol - enforcers of Dictat Bureaucratica

Parchment Patrollers - paper shufflers, minions of the office ("peepers")

Peek, Lord (a Bellicose henchman responsible for castle information security)

Peeper - Parchment Patroller

PETs (Personal Enhancement Techniques) = private program of lords providing selected vassals special training and prerogatives

Piles, Prince of the (Crown Prince and leader of the stables from the Tower of Feculence)

PIT - Primarily Inactive Team (a TQM group)

Plans and Bans, Tower of (Lord of Futilities) = where castle planning is supposed to take place

Plumbing and Stalling, Tower of = castle workshop (Lord of the Ductwork)

Power, Tower of (King's Tower - where Lancelot is)

Princepals (Lords of Stables)

Pot Raid - Purchase Request (PR)

R&D (Rework and Diddle) - research and development

Reap, Lord of (Tower of Collections)

Reformation = reorganization

Rod, Lord of the (Prince of Power's Chief of Staff)

Rubble, Tower of

Saddamn Ibn Sain - leader of the barbarians from The Middle Muddle

SAVE (Special Advisory Vassal Element)

SAVEiors (reformation vassals; members of SAVE)

Shocked, Knights = Marines

Shucktray (ashtray)

SNOB (Senior Nobles' Order of Bosses)

Stable, East - Lord Sir Howard Fleetsmile
Stable, West - Lord Sir Rodney Longnose

Stable, North - Lord Sir Leslie Slimelips
Stable, South - Lord Sir Linus Limpwrist

STAFFS (Special Taskers of All Foolish Fiefdom Silliness)

Stewards of the Stalls (middle management)

Super Watcher Tower = built for Great Salad Oil War
(improvement on old Watcher Tower)

Tekees - the working peasants

TESTs, Total Empire Specification Tables (requirements)

Thomas à Bucket - factotum to Sir Lancelot in Tower of Power

Tidings, Tower of (marketing)

Tours, Tower of (Travel Tower)

Transubstantiation (Ennobling as a lord)

Transitory Comprehensions = lesson learned

Universe (Job-finding program) - also known as "The Lottery")

Vassals - supervisors and middle management

VETO, Tower of (Vocationally Equal Tradesmen Opportunities)

Vice-Lord = Deputy lord

Watcher Center - the around-the-clock room in the Watcher Tower

Watcher Tower (where around the clock surveillance in protection
of the castle takes place)

Whip, Lord of the

Wise Men (Smoke and Mirrors; also known as Fog and Smog)